WHEN
PEOPLE
PRAY

What Happens When Ordinary People
Pray to An Extraordinary God

BRIAN ALARID
WITH HOLDEN HILL

CEDAR GATE
PUBLISHING

WHENPEOPLEPRAY.COM

CEDAR GATE PUBLISHING
www.cedargtepublishing.com

PRAISE FOR *WHEN PEOPLE PRAY*

"God has His hand all over Brian Alarid and his message on prayer. There is no way you can read this book and not want to immediately get down on your knees and begin praying like you never have before. There is no question that America desperately needs prayer, and prayer unlike it has received in a long while. I believe this book may go far in meeting that need."

—Richard Blackaby
President, Blackaby Ministries, co-author of Experiencing God

"*When People Pray* reads like it came off the pages of the book of Acts. Many of us long for the amazing encounters that unfold in the first century Christian movement. The church not only saw millions of people come into a relationship with God, but their prayer and presence changed the very culture and fabric of the cities they entered. Brian's story reminds us that it is not only still possible today, but it is actually happening all over the world. So moved by this book, the pastors and leaders I serve alongside are bringing this movement to our city."

—Randy Frazee
Pastor & Author of His Mighty Strength

"Brian Alarid's voice and leadership are a powerful addition to the burgeoning global 24-7 prayer movement. This scalable model focuses on city transformation, which has proven successful in Brian's own city, Albuquerque, New Mexico, where he is much respected and well-loved across denominational divides. This book is both inspiring and practical, and I pray that it will equip leaders in every field to greater faith in united prayer."

—Pete Greig
Founder, 24-7 Prayer International

"I was so touched and impacted by *When People Pray*. By combining his story, the stories of others, and the wisdom of godly men and women, Brian helps you understand the call and reality of prayer. You will never be sorry that you read this book and, like me, will have a hard time putting it down as God speaks through Brian to your heart."

—Morgan Jackson
Senior Vice President, Faith Comes By Hearing

"During my tenure as Lt. Governor of New Mexico, it was a privilege to build a personal friendship and partnership with Brian Alarid that continues even now that I am back in the private sector as the CEO of our family business. I have witnessed firsthand the power and transformation of united prayer and service through the movement that Brian leads and so eloquently describes in his book, *When People Pray*. I have been blessed to have Brian pray with me and my wife Debra on many occasions, and I know that you will be incredibly blessed by this powerful book. I encourage everyone to read it."

—John Sanchez
Former Lt. Governor of New Mexico

"It has been an absolute pleasure partnering with Pastor Brian Alarid and New Mexico Prays on initiatives to help move Albuquerque forward. The success we have seen through our partnership on Convoy of Hope and Love ABQ has made a huge impact on our city."

—Tim Keller
Mayor of Albuquerque, New Mexico

"I first met Brian Alarid when he reached out to me as police chief and offered to be a partner in prayer for the city and my police department. Since then, I have seen him faithfully in action ministering to my officers and the community. And we have seen growth and life in areas never opened before throughout the city. The city government has since welcomed more faith partnerships through the work Brian has built. Brian's life and ministry are examples of prayer and faith in action. I found his book to be inspirational and a source of spiritual encouragement for me both on a professional and personal level. I am honored to work with Brian and have him as a friend."

—Mike Geier
Chief of Police, Albuquerque, New Mexico

"In his book, *When People Pray,* my dear friend Rev. Brian Alarid leads us down the path of prayer in this accessible, stirring, and inspirational work. As he opens up his heart to us in these pages, Brian leads us to the heart of Jesus Christ, who is the breath, substance, and ultimate goal of all prayer. Whether you are a 'prayer warrior' or someone who has been longing to hear the voice of God, you will find comfort, challenge, and confirmation here that the 'Hound of Heaven' wants nothing more than to express His love for you in the quiet and prayerful recesses of your soul. I am grateful to Brian for this gift to all of us, and I pray that many will turn these pages often and reverently as they draw ever closer to the living God whose own prayerful breath brought us into being."

—Most Reverend John C. Wester

Archbishop, Archdiocese of Santa Fe

"I have known Brian Alarid always to be a man of passion. Even the church he founded is called Passion. Through traumatic events, God found a way to direct those passions into having His people talk to Him 24/7/365 globally. *When People Pray* will stir you in ways you've never been stirred before. Individuals, communities, and even nations are being transformed by *When People Pray.* May your life be impacted by Brian's transparency and message as mine has. You'll want every person in your church to read *When People Pray.*"

—Sam Chand

Leadership Consultant and author of The Sequence to Success

"Prayer does not inform God of our desires; it aligns our heart and path with His. Brian guides readers on this joyful journey whose destination is beyond anything we can think or imagine but as close as a prayer."

—Kathy Branzell

President, National Day of Prayer Task Force

"Brian's story will move you, capture your heart, and give you revelation into your own God-designed journey. You will be brought into a modern-day move of the Holy Spirit that's starting to sweep America and soon the whole Earth! This book is about you, Brian, and every one of us who is alive in this remarkable hour. Read, weep, and be inspired by this powerful story!"

—Mark Anderson

President, call2all, YWAM Kansas City

"My good friend Brian Alarid is a living, breathing embodiment of his new book, *When People Pray*. This guy lives and breathes prayer. What I especially love is his passion to help the Church grow in this critical area of ministry. *When People Pray* is going to spark a movement of prayer in the Body of Christ!"

—Dr. David Butts

Chairman, America's National Prayer Committee

"God is on the move throughout our country, calling people to pray! In dozens of cities, the Church is uniting around prayer, serving the community, and evangelism in a way I've never seen before. *When People Pray* provides great encouragement and practical help for all who long to see renewal come to the Church and the Church acting as one in their city."

—Kevin Palau

President, Luis Palau Association

"Brian Alarid's book *When People Pray* is very exciting and is a huge edification to people who pray. It is an encouragement for people who wish to pray and don't know quite how to pray. It is a motivator for people who desire to take intercessory prayer seriously. I am blessed by Brian's integrity and transparency."

—Leslie Keegel

Global Chairman, Foursquare Church

"This book is not only a timely resource and tool, it is also a reminder of the transforming power of prayer. Brian Alarid, with a prophetic clarity, provokes us to individual knee posture and a corporate agreement that will awaken the heart of the church to bring healing to the soul of communities and even the nation. Brian shares through a paradigm of personal experience, including his own share of trials, but the outcome was a call to prayer with a deeper heart, passion, and understanding. Recognizing that prayer is so much more than handing a list of requests and petitions to God, Brian reminds us that prayer is an actual surrender to the Father's will, no matter the outcome. I highly recommend this book. It is filled with real life testimonies that will encourage you in your own journey and heart cry for your life and in your community."

—Doug Stringer

President, Somebody Cares International

"Seldom these days do you find a fresh perspective on the ancient practice, example, and admonition to pray, but get ready to be surprised, stretched, and blessed! Brian has intertwined the power of story with the simplicity of prayer insights from each chapter to provide a road map for deepened intimacy with the Lord. Read it, engage with it, and reap great reward."

—Dr. David Ferguson

Executive Director, Great Commandment Network

"My brother Brian's book, *When People Pray*, carries weight because Brian is a man of prayer. Brian and Mercy's home is a house of prayer, and their children are prayer warriors. Out of an intimate relationship with the Lord flows this book. I believe this book will be the impetus for a prayer movement that will lead to the greatest global awakening in history."

—John Alarid

Senior Pastor, Freedom City Church

"Brian has written a heartfelt book from his perspective of how God works in the world when we pray. More importantly, he also addresses the question of how we individually and collectively respond to the results of the prayers we make—on behalf of others and ourselves. We are reminded that prayer is a powerful faith-based approach to addressing human conditions that we do not fully understand, because it gives us access to God who does understand. All prayers are answered—although perhaps not as we would have it, but as God would have it. What we do with the results of prayer is God's way of involving us in His Word for what improves our human existence. Listen not to the literal words that Brian says, but 'for what the words say to you.' This book should give everyone valuable insight on what that means when people pray."

—Dr. David E. Peercy
Retired Distinguished Senior Scientist, Sandia National Laboratories

"I know of no one better to author this book than Brian Alarid. Brian's passion is clear and his devotion to see prayer in the ranks of leadership from the top down has been a driving factor in America Prays. State by state and country by country, Brian's passion to see the hand of God working globally is amazing to watch. This book, *When People Pray,* is the next logical step because it reveals the power of prayer to individuals and families, encouraging them to seek God in heaven and all that He is capable of. Brian is not only a great leader, but a prayer warrior inspired to pen this book that others may know the power of when people pray."

—Gregg Hull
Mayor of Rio Rancho, New Mexico

"I want to personally thank Brian Alarid for writing *When People Pray.* I found it challenging, encouraging, inspirational and extremely timely. Brian brings two powerful weapons to this book. First, he is an exceptional writer and easy to read. Second and more importantly, he has a breadth of understanding and experience in prayer. Together those two ingredients make *When People Pray* an outstanding rallying cry for the urgency of prayer. Brian has seen significant answers to prayer, both personally and corporately. The way he shares those experiences and answers makes me want to not only pray more, but pray better. If you're interested in upping your game in prayer and learning to gain increased power and confidence when talking to God, then *When People Pray* is for you."

—Will Davis Jr.
Founder & Senior Pastor, Austin Christian Fellowship

*I dedicate this book to my wife
and the great love of my life, Mercy*

*Your honesty challenges me
Your grace restores me
Your courage inspires me
Your touch melts me
Your beauty captivates me
Your strength upholds me
Your wisdom guides me
Your prayers sustain me
Your love transforms me*

*I want to spend eternity with you and
never let you out of my sight
not even for one second.
You're my best friend, my true love,
my everything
And you have no equal.*

ACKNOWLEDGMENTS

I want to honor the person who was the inspiration behind this book. **Jesus,** you are my Lord, my Savior, my best friend, and my first love. All this is because of you and for you. By your grace, I'll love you and serve you all the days of my life.

Mercy, you have poured your soul into me and this book. You are my life, my love, my everything.

Chloe, Colin, and Lauren, you are the greatest gifts God has ever given me. No father has ever been more proud of his children. I adore you and treasure you. I look forward to worshipping Jesus with you in the ages to come.

Carla Heinecke, you have always been my biggest fan and loudest cheerleader. I love you, Mom.

Bruno Interlandi, thank you for your unwavering support and friendship. You believed in me when I didn't believe in myself. You are the best friend a man could ever have.

Trey Kent, Jason Hubbard, Dave Butts, and Lewis Hogan, thank you for serving with me on the Board of America Prays. It's a joy to do life and ministry with you.

Holden Hill, thank you for helping me write my story and express so eloquently the passion and vision inside my heart. You have brought out the best in me every step of the way. I hope Jesus allows us to collaborate on many books.

Anna McHargue, thank you for editing this book and bringing your expertise to this project. I am forever indebted to you.

Richard Mansfield, David Cooper, John Robb, Danny Sanchez, Nate Heitzig, Mike Dickenson, Ray Montoya, Jason Dickenson, and Vince Torres, thank you for helping me birth and lead New Mexico Prays. Your example of humility and devotion laid the foundation for this movement.

Ed and Elizabeth Horne, thank you for helping me birth America Prays in your home, for loving me, believing in me, and giving me the courage to take a leap of faith. Thank you for investing generously into America Prays.

Brian and Marla Hill, thank you for your friendship, love, and generosity. You exemplify Jesus' command to love your neighbor as yourself. I cherish your friendship.

Passion Church, thank you for the honor of serving as your pastor. Your love has shaped me and inspired me.

Dick Eastman, thank you for being a friend, mentor, adviser, and spiritual father to me. Thank you for teaching me and millions of believers how to pray more effectively.

CONTENTS

DICK EASTMAN

We can't possibly know all there is to know about prayer, but we all have heard the stories of God-on-the-move as He responds to the prayers of His people. When we spend time opening our hearts in the presence of the Lord, we begin to experience the transformation that begins from the place of prayer. *When People Pray* is an account of just that: what happens when people *actually* pray.

When People Pray is an invitation to experience prayer afresh for ourselves. **I'm totally serious when I say this is one of the most significant books on prayer I've read in my lifetime.**

In reflecting on Brian Alarid's unique journey into a calling of prayer (that could well lead to one of history's greatest prayer movements), I couldn't help but look back on my own journey of prayer. I believed in prayer, taught and preached on prayer, and had even written my first book on prayer—all without actually having a consistent, daily prayer habit.

It was not that I didn't pray—it was that I was much more of what some might describe as a "crisis" pray-er. I prayed when urgent situations called for prayer. (I prayed a lot during those early days because God let me encounter a multitude of crisis situations to keep me praying.) I had been an ordained minister for seven years before I actually understood the transforming power of prayer.

Similarly, God took Brian Alarid on his own journey, one that revealed to him that prayer—especially united prayer of churches of all denominations in cities across our nation (and even around the world)—could transform whole communities and ultimately entire nations.

This journey, along with the visionary impact of other key prayer leaders with a similar vision, led Brian to give his leadership to a powerful movement of prayer in our nation called America Prays. I'll let him tell the story, though I will convey that in my lifetime as a prayer mobilizer, I know of nothing that could more radically impact our nation for Jesus than the vision of America Prays.

In a nutshell, America Prays is seeing churches of every conceivable denomination unite in a profoundly simple strategy to sustain 24/7 united prayer in every community of every size across the landscape of America. The strategy is so simple that it can work anywhere. And I totally agree, as Brian shares in this book, "Only a united church can heal a divided nation."

You need to read about this vision in the pages that follow. Indeed, you may be the very person who will carry this flame into your city, town, or community. But it must begin with pastors. If you're not a pastor, you most likely have one. Read this book and then buy a copy and give it to your pastor as soon as you can.

Already Brian's vision for America Prays has led to an expansion of the vision to World Prays. That's because what God is doing to spread this vision in America will easily work in any nation on Earth—and it's already happening. Prayer can happen anywhere!

If you want to read something that is profoundly prophetic— read this book. The vision you read on these pages, I believe, is destined to happen. To me, it's only a matter of time. And it could well lead to a worldwide revival.

Let me just add, the story Brian shares in the following pages is both compelling and tender. He takes you on a journey from the hospital bedside of his daughter, to the halls of his high school, to the streets in prayer. He shares vulnerably from his own wrestling with the Lord and the calling on his life along the way.

I know Brian's story well because he is one of only a few leaders in my lifetime who has joined me in entire days of prayer together. On multiple occasions, Brian has driven five hours from his home in Albuquerque to our headquarters in Colorado Springs just to spend a day in prayer with me.

As you read these pages, you will be encouraged and equipped in practical ways for a life of prayer. You will be challenged to hear and respond to the voice of God in your heart, perhaps as never before. And trust me—God will speak to you through these pages.

Brian's experiences will expand your imagination and grow your vision for the power of Jesus and the possibility in prayer. You will be left not simply with more information about prayer, but with a multiplied desire to dive deeper into your personal story of prayer. You will especially learn a powerful truth Brian shares in these pages that "prayer is more about the object of prayer, Jesus, than it is about the outcome of prayer."

I am honored to partner with Brian, his strategy, and the ministry of both America Prays and World Prays. Our ministry, Every Home for Christ, has truly embraced this vision as our own. I believe this movement that was birthed in pain on the floor of a hopeless hospital room will grow to cover the whole Earth, spreading the hope of eternal salvation in Jesus Christ. Don't miss having your personal part in this extraordinary world-changing vision.

—Dick Eastman
International President, Every Home for Christ
President, America's National Prayer Committee

PREFACE

*History belongs to the intercessors—those who
believe and pray the future into being.*[1]

Walter Wink

So, *what happens when people pray?*

That question has gripped my heart since I was a young man.

What happens when *you* pray? And I'm not just referring to the effect of your prayers on others or situations. What happens to *you* when you pray?

What happens when a man, woman, youth, or child pauses to pray to the God of Heaven?

What happens when a student invites God to invade their school campus?

What happens when couples and families pray together?

What happens when business owners seek God for creative ideas to generate wealth and impact others?

What happens when a city or state unites in prayer?

What happens when a nation cries out to God?

What could happen when every country and people group on the planet are covered in day and night prayer?

Through the pages and stories that follow, I'll take you on a fast-paced, sometimes slow, often painful, and many times hilarious journey of what happens when people pray.

But as gripping and exciting as the stories you read may be, only you can discover what can happen when YOU pray. I hope this book becomes a primer to the grand story that will be written when you pray and God answers.

—Brian Alarid

Don't worry about anything; instead, pray about everything.
Tell God what you need and thank him for all he has done.
Then you will experience God's peace, which exceeds anything we
can understand. His peace will guard your hearts and minds as you
live in Christ Jesus.

—*Philippians 4:6-7 (NLT)*

Prayer...is the root, the fountain, the mother of a thousand
blessings.[2]

—*St. Chrysostom*

The priority of prayer is found in one way or another on almost
every page of the Bible and in every chapter of church history. It is
neither a peripheral theme nor an optional extra for the desperate
and the devout. It does not belong to some other time in history,
not to some other type of person more spiritual or disciplined or
experienced than you and me. Prayer is nothing at all unless it is a
matter of vast and all-consuming importance for each one of us.[3]

—*Pete Greig*

What the Church needs today is not more machinery or better, not
new organizations or more and novel methods, but men whom the
Holy Ghost can use—men of prayer, men mighty in prayer. The
Holy Ghost does not flow through methods, but through men. He
does not come on machinery, but on men. He does not anoint plans,
but men—men of prayer.[4]

—*E. M. Bounds*

Prayer will make a man cease from sin, or sin will entice a man to
cease from prayer.[5]

—*John Bunyan*

CHAPTER 1

HELPLESS

"**G**od, don't take my little girl. Please don't take her. Please, God!"

With both fists knotted and eyes blood-shot, I silently pleaded with God. I would say I prayed, except that I'm not sure such frantic fury qualifies as prayer. I managed to keep my mouth shut.

My twelve-year-old daughter lay motionless on the large hospital bed, where she had been for weeks.

"Mr. and Mrs. Alarid, your daughter has stroke-like symptoms. The left side of her body is unresponsive, and her eyelids won't open unassisted. We're doing everything we can for her, but even if she recovers, she may never walk again."

My wife, Mercy, had to leave to teach a class at our local community college, and I was all alone with my daughter. I contemplated the rest of what the doctor said.

"You should know that Chloe has also sustained crippling nerve pain. We would give her pain meds, but she appears to be allergic to the only medication that could help. The best thing we can do now is to monitor her condition."

"Jesus, please," I muttered.

I stood still for what seemed like ages. Finally, stepping closer, I traced the soft line of my daughter's cheek with my hand. Using my thumb and index finger, I pulled back the lids of her brown eyes so she could see me.

"I love you, Chloe. You're going to make it. Jesus is going to heal you, baby," I whispered.

Chloe's eyes swam, searching the room but not settling on anything in particular.

"Chloe, can you hear me?"

Then, her eyes settled on me. Even as I wondered how things could get any worse, I knew that, somehow, they had.

"I… I, Chloe?" she asked.

Needles of ice sank into my heart. I stood frozen, refusing to acknowledge what I had just heard.

She can't remember who she is?

I nearly screamed for the doctor, but I couldn't. My voice trembled as I whispered again.

"Chloe, do you know who I am?"

Chloe stared into my eyes.

"You…Dada. You…you love me."

My heart shattered, and any denial I had about Chloe's condition was instantly overridden by my desperate need to save her.

"Someone help! Chloe doesn't know who she is!"

Several nurses burst into the room. For the next hour, I watched things happen in a distant haze. I watched the neurologist enter the room, test Chloe, and ask me question after question. Chloe was suffering from complete amnesia, and I was the only memory she had left.

When the neurologist finally left to review her tests, I stumbled to a corner of the room and collapsed to my knees. I trembled with fear.

Like shadows on the wall, I remembered a nightmare I had years before Chloe was born. In the dream, Mercy and I had a beautiful daughter who died of a rare disease at the age of twelve. I prayed when I woke up, "God, if you're going to give us a daughter just to take her away, I don't want to have her."

I battled my fear in the aftermath of the dream, killed it, and buried its carcass in the ground. But now, my fear was back with a vengeance. So, I vented my pain and anger at God. "Jesus, I told you I didn't want to have a daughter if you were going to take her away! I told you!"

But there was no answer. As my fury mounted, I opened my mouth wide in a silent scream and broke into uncontrollable tears. I fell to my face on the floor and prayed once more.

"Jesus, please promise me that Chloe is not going to die. I don't care how long it takes for her to recover and learn to walk again. Just don't take my baby girl from me."

I listened with my head on the floor and my soul broken. And I heard a voice, not a voice like thunder, but a gentle whisper in my heart.

"Start 24/7 prayer, and I'll take care of Chloe."

I remained still for a long time, unable to move and afraid to respond. I knew all too well what God was asking. The vision of America covered in prayer, twenty-four hours a day, seven days a week, had been on my heart for decades. But now I rebelled against it, feeling like God was twisting the knife already protruding from my chest.

"What?" I nearly laughed. The silence that followed was answer enough.

"No!" I bit off. But that single word didn't seem satisfactory, so I continued.

"Jesus, have you bothered to look down here? My daughter hasn't been able to walk for weeks. She can't move the left side of her body, open her eyelids, or even remember who she is. And you want me to start a prayer movement in the middle of this? No way!

"And you know what else? Look, I'm praying right now. I've been crying out to you all this time, praying that you would heal Chloe. And what have you done?"

I laughed bitterly.

"I've been praying that my daughter would get better, but instead, she's getting worse. Don't you realize that I'm probably the worst person on the planet right now to stand up, rally people to you, and proclaim 'prayer works?' No, God! Find someone else."

As I continued to rant, God's proposal only grew louder. I knew there was no way out—only through—but I resisted all the same. Minutes turned into hours.

I wrestled with God the whole night, and with dawn close at hand, I did the only thing I was still capable of—I surrendered.

"Jesus, please take care of Chloe. With your help, I'll start 24/7 prayer in Albuquerque."

But that didn't encompass the scope of God's request. And like a horse feels the gentle pull of its rider, my heart felt God's stirring.

"Not only Albuquerque, Brian, but the whole state. And not only New Mexico, but all of America. And not only America. I want you to start a movement that covers every city, every state, and every nation in day and night prayer until I return."

Game over.

Starting unceasing prayer in Albuquerque seemed daunting enough, but this—this was insanity. My heart was broken, my emotions were fried, and my faith had never been weaker. I was in no condition to start anything, much less a prayer movement.

I knew Jesus was real, and I loved Him deeply. But how could I rally people across the globe to believe in the power of prayer when I was struggling to believe my prayers for my daughter would even work?

"If you help me, Father, I'll obey you," I prayed.

WHERE'S THE POWER?

My parents taught me to believe in the power of prayer. Today, I hear the same message in churches, on the radio, in songs, in movies, on social media and blogs, and everywhere else Christians proclaim it—"There is power in prayer."

After all, we read as much in John 14:13 when Jesus tells His disciples, "Whatever you ask in my name, this I will do, that the Father may be glorified in the Son." But as I cried out to God for my daughter, I started to wonder if I had misunderstood prayer all this time. And now, four years later, I don't just wonder—I know for sure.

There is no power in prayer—not a single drop.

What? The author of a book on prayer and the leader of a prayer movement just said prayer is powerless?

Yes, I did! Prayer can't change things any more than you can drive a set of car keys.

Now, before you burn me in effigy, let me explain.

Although I no longer believe in the power of prayer, I have never believed more in the power of *Jesus* to answer the prayers of simple, ordinary people.

Like a car key, prayer is powerless on its own. All a key does is turn the ignition. That's what gives you access to the real power source—the engine. In the same way, prayer gives you access to the presence and power of God. But don't for one second be tempted to think the power is in your prayer—the power is in Jesus.

God designed it that way so that only He can receive the glory from answered prayer. Your prayers give you access to Jesus, who is your intercessor. He is seated at the right hand of the Father and is praying for you (Romans 8:34).

> *Prayer is powerless on its own, but it gives you access to Jesus, who is the power of God. Put your faith in Jesus, not in prayer.*

Put your faith in Jesus, not in prayer. Jesus is the power of God (1 Corinthians 1:24). Jesus said when He rose from the dead in Matthew 28:18, "All power is given unto me in heaven and on earth."

The message of faith often preached in America focuses on portions of Scripture like this one in Hebrews 11:33-35:

"Who through faith conquered kingdoms, administered justice, and gained what was promised; who shut the mouths of lions, quenched the raging fire, and escaped the edge of the sword; who gained strength from weakness, became mighty in battle, and put foreign armies to flight. Women received back their dead, raised to life again."

The implication is that if you have faith, you will always win. You will always come out on top, always succeed, and never experience loss. If only the author of the epistle to the Hebrews had stopped there, right? But the Holy Spirit inspired him to continue writing to give us a more complete picture of what faith looks like, explaining in Hebrews 11:35-40:

"...Others were tortured and refused their release, so that they might gain a better resurrection. Still others endured mocking and flogging, and even chains and imprisonment.

They were stoned, they were sawed in two, they were put to death by the sword. They went around in sheepskins and goatskins, destitute, oppressed, and mistreated.

The world was not worthy of them. They wandered in deserts and mountains and hid in caves and holes in the ground.

These were all commended for their faith, yet they did not receive what was promised. God had planned something better for us, so that together with us they would be made perfect."

Sometimes serving Jesus means you will be tortured, mocked, flogged, and imprisoned. Just ask believers in Iran and North Korea.

Sometimes serving Jesus means you will be stoned, sawed in half, or killed.

Sometimes serving Jesus means you will be destitute, oppressed, mistreated, or homeless.

Sometimes serving Jesus will cost you something, maybe even everything. But don't you dare feel bad for yourself. Salvation was free to you, but it wasn't free for the giver, and it wasn't cheap. Loving you cost God everything He had—it cost Him the life of Jesus, His one and only Son.

By all means, please pray. Pray anytime, everywhere, about everything. Pray always. Pray in faith, pray fervently, pray passionately. But never forget that prayer is more about the object of prayer—Jesus—than it is about the outcome of prayer. And that's why we pray: because **Jesus is worthy** (Revelation 5:8).

> *Prayer is more about the object of prayer—Jesus—than it is about the outcome of prayer.*

Prayer is all about Jesus. Although prayer is powerless, Jesus is all-powerful. There's nothing God can't do for you. When you are down to nothing, God is up to something!

That's what I would come to learn. But as I lay exhausted in the hospital, my heart was still ruled more by anguish than peace. I was scared, angry, and brokenhearted. And I didn't want to be alone. I called Morgan Jackson, the Senior Vice President of Faith Comes By Hearing. He's been one of my closest friends and mentors for the past sixteen years. And right then, I needed him more than ever. When Morgan arrived, he confiscated both my cell phones.

"I called your associate pastor. He agreed to preach tomorrow, and I told him to let people know you aren't receiving visitors today. Now, you're going to go over to that corner and take a nap on the couch. I'll take care of Chloe."

What? Nobody puts Baby in a corner.[6] "Morgan, I can't sleep when Chloe…" Morgan interrupted me before I could finish my sentence.

"Yes, you can, and you will. Your body needs rest. Go lie down right now and fall asleep. I've got Chloe. Don't worry."

Are you kidding me? How do I not worry?

I didn't want to concede, but Morgan was more than a friend—he was the most trusted mentor of my life. He was my Yoda, and I knew I had zero chance of changing his mind.

Skywalker yielded.

As I drifted off to sleep praying for my daughter, I remembered a time years ago when God answered the prayers of my godly mother.

CHAPTER 2

HOMECOMING

W ith a final shove, I stuffed my books into my backpack and slung it over my shoulder. I was about to turn sixteen, and it was the Friday before homecoming, fall 1990.

"Brian!"

I turned to the sound of my name. My best friend, also named Bryan, was weaving his way through the classroom toward me.

"Are you ready for homecoming next week?" Bryan asked with a mischievous grin.

I matched it and clapped his hand.

"You know it!"

"You and Susan are still coming with us, right?" Bryan asked.

I nodded.

"Yeah. We'll be at your house for pictures before and then come back with you guys after the dance."

Then I asked, "Did you really get a limousine?"

Bryan's grin widened.

"You better believe it! And even better than that, my parents are going to be out of town Friday night, so…"

Bryan winked, suggesting the rest.

"That's what's up!"

I smiled with my lips, but my soul revolted against his obvious implications.

That evening and Saturday flew by. Next thing I knew, it was Sunday and a unique one at that. I was in the kitchen, making a sandwich and fumbling through the refrigerator for mayo. I heard the back door open and footsteps near the kitchen.

"Look at you, making your own breakfast."

I turned to the sound of my mother's voice. She smiled at me, and I smiled back.

"I can't find the mayo. Do you know where it's at?"

Mom peeked inside the fridge door beside me and immediately found it, obviously to my amazement.

How do moms do that?

"Thanks," I replied as I spread the mayo on the bread.

"Can you come to church with me this morning?" she asked.

I took a bite of my sandwich and turned toward my bedroom.

"No, thanks, I'm good," I mumbled through a mouth full.

"Come on, honey. You haven't been to church in...well, I don't know how long."

"Church is so lame, Mom! Sorry. I'm not going."

I could tell she was sad when she left the house alone, but I went back to my room, nonetheless, to finish my sandwich. Then, as the stereo played my favorite songs, I dozed off to sleep.

Two hours later, I woke up to the startling sound of someone banging on our front door. I jumped out of bed and bolted toward the sound.

There was Michael, one of my mom's friends from church, giving me *the look* through the glass door. Since my parents were divorced and I was living in Northern California with my mom, Michael had taken me on as a younger brother. I liked him, but the moment I saw him at my front door, I knew war was at hand. I was glad the door was locked.

Michael's voice boomed like thunder through the walls of my house.

"Brian, open the door. You're coming to church with me whether you like it or not!"

"Nice try, Michael! But I'm staying right here."

"If you don't come out here, I'll break the door down and drag you out."

I considered that for a moment. Michael was tall, broad, and strong, but I didn't think he would break down the door. I called his bluff.

"No, you won't."

"Why do you think I brought this?" Michael asked as he held up some rope. "If you don't open the door in the next ten seconds, I'm going to break the lock, hog-tie you, and carry you to the front row of the church over my shoulder."

Then, Michael started counting.

With three seconds left, I unlocked the door and stepped out. I peered up into Michael's face.

"You win," I mumbled. I wasn't quite sure Michael would follow through with his threat, but I did not want to find out.

Michael grinned and slapped me on the back.

"Smart move!"

We drove to the basketball-gym-turned-church, and I grudgingly sat at the back where my mind could drift without anyone noticing too much.

Some people don't like going to church because they feel like it's full of hypocrites. I, on the other hand, didn't want to go because I knew that if I did, I would *be* the hypocrite. In my mind, I would be just another kid who pretended to be a Christian on Sunday but didn't live like one the rest of the week.

Instead of focusing on the message, I daydreamed about homecoming Friday night. I didn't think about the pictures, the limousine, dinner, or even the dance. No, my thoughts were saturated with one relentless, intoxicating, lustful idea.

"What if, after the dance, when we get back to the house, Susan and I are by ourselves and…"

With an explosion of rage, the half of me that still loved Jesus revolted against my fantasy.

"Get a grip, Brian! What are you doing? Are you going to break your vow to remain a virgin until marriage?"

My flesh, furious at my conviction, shot back.

"What do you mean, 'What are you doing?' It's obvious, isn't it? I'm having fun! What's wrong with having a little fun while you're in high school?"

"You seriously think that?" My conviction mocked back. "Oh, come on, Brian! God called you according to His purpose—a purpose far greater and fulfilling than the lust you're entertaining. Or don't you remember?"

My flesh laughed mockingly inside my mind.

"Oh, I remember, alright. I remember praying my heart out night after night that God would heal Mom and Dad's marriage. I remember going to a thousand church services before the age of ten and seeing nothing but empty and fake people. Yes, I remember all too well."

Seething, my flesh waited for my soul's response. When it came, it was gentle.

"And yet, you've forgotten God."

Just then, the pastor caught my attention. "I'm going off notes for a minute. The Spirit is putting a word on my heart for a young man here. He wasn't in the first service, but he's here now."

The pastor scanned the crowd, looking for whoever the young man might be.

"Here's what the Lord says to you: You're going to make a terrible decision this week that is going to take you on a twenty-year detour. Two nights ago, you were lying on your bed, and you said to God, 'I finally have everything I ever wanted. So, why do I still feel empty and alone?'"

I felt the hair on my arms stand on end. How could he possibly know that? No one should have known because when I uttered those words two nights ago, they had been in my head.

"I don't know who you are or what you're running from, but God is saying to come up here right now. You need to repent and come back to Jesus."

I remained frozen in my seat.

"Brian, I think he's talking about you," my friend Tammy whispered in my ear.

But I didn't respond. Behind my glazed-over eyes, a war raged. I believed in Jesus, but I wasn't living for Him, and I knew it. And because I knew it, I would feel like a hypocrite if I went down that aisle to meet the pastor. My repentance would be fake, and I refused to be fake.

My friend insisted, "Brian, I think he's talking to you."

No way, I thought sarcastically.

Then my other friend, Maggie, joined in.

"Come on, Brian. I'll walk down with you."

I would have rolled my eyes if not for Tammy's sincere expression. I stood up, albeit against my will, and shuffled out of the row. Tammy held my right arm and Maggie, my left.

There could be worse ways to walk toward an altar, I said to myself.

With every step, the war in my soul intensified. I wanted to serve Jesus, but I also wanted to indulge in my flesh. I wanted to give myself to God's calling for me, but the lure of the world called louder.

Having almost reached the pastor, I contemplated a simple solution in my head—a solution as stupid as any man has ever conceived. With my jaw set and mind decided, I told God how it was going to be.

"God, I'll serve you…"

I watched my foot cross the free throw line on the basketball court, where I made my living as a point guard.

"…but not yet."

And just like that, I collapsed on the gym's shiny wooden floor as if someone had whacked me with a baseball bat.

I didn't know my mother had been praying for me to return to Jesus for several months. Now, God had walked into the room to answer her prayer.

My world went black.

CHAPTER 3

SURRENDER

🔥

"**B**rian, wake up! Look!" Mercy's excited voice jolted me out of my sleep.

It was two days after my night-long conversation with God on the hospital floor.

"What?" I blurted, squinting my eyes and scanning Chloe's hospital room. Then, I saw.

Chloe, who was never supposed to stand again, was walking across the room on her own two feet. I gawked.

"Daddy, I can walk by myself!" Chloe shouted when she reached the wall.

I beamed. "That's amazing, sweetheart. Let me see you do that again."

And she did. And then again and again.

While my heart rejoiced, it also broke with sorrow seeing this beautiful girl, who only weeks before had owned the basketball court, now stumble across the room like a newborn fawn. But at least she was walking.

And as her memory started to come back and her left side functions returned to normal, we decided to take her home against the wishes of her doctors. On May 16, 2016, my daughter walked out of the hospital with her arms swinging at her sides. That was two whole days after the neurologist told us she would never walk again.

I wish I could say the story ended there, and we all lived happily ever after. But you know better.

Twenty-five minutes later, Chloe was screaming in pain as we pulled into our garage. I fought back pangs of emotion and forced myself to move. With Mercy close beside me, I carried Chloe to our bed and pulled the covers over her.

As I sat beside her and listened to her sob, I prayed in silence.

Jesus, please. Please! We need you right now. Help us!

But things only got worse.

In a matter of weeks, Chloe's condition regressed. She developed hypersensitivity to sound and light and became prone to severe migraines. Her motor skills had suffered, so Mercy and I took turns spoon-feeding her during mealtimes. And if all that wasn't enough, her sporadic waves of pain forced her back into a wheelchair, or on good days, crutches.

At times, it felt like I could barely breathe. I prayed God would heal Chloe, and by His grace, she walked out of the hospital. But now, she was fighting for her life again. That made it difficult for us to pray.

Maybe you've felt this way before.

Sometimes we don't feel like praying. A soldier doesn't always feel like training or going into combat. But what matters is that you show up for duty. It's the same with prayer. Showing up for prayer is half the battle.

Prayer alone has the power to move the hand of God on your behalf. The devil knows how dangerous prayer makes you to the darkness, so he will do everything in his power to discourage and distract you from prayer.

Samuel Chadwick explains: "The one concern of the devil is to keep Christians from praying. He fears nothing from prayerless studies, prayerless work and prayerless religion. He laughs at our toil, mocks at our wisdom, but he trembles when we pray."[7]

Prayer is not like going on a family picnic—it is warfare. Prayer is a declaration of war against our enemy, the devil. It's a battle between kingdoms. As my friend Brian Hill says,

> **PRAYER IS WARFARE.**
>
> *The two most powerful weapons you have in your arsenal are prayer and God's Word.*

"Prayer is your first line of offense against the enemy, not your last line of defense."

Paul lays it out for us in Ephesians 6:11-12: "Put on the full armor of God, so that you can make your stand against the devil's schemes. For our struggle is not against flesh and blood, but against the rulers, against the authorities, against the powers of this world's darkness, and against the spiritual forces of evil in the heavenly realms."

The two most powerful weapons you have in your arsenal are prayer and God's Word. Every time the devil attacked Him during His forty-day fast in the wilderness, Jesus responded with Scripture.

As my disappointment with God spiraled dangerously out of control, Jesus confronted me with one simple but profound truth—**His grace was more than enough for me.**

One day, Jesus is going to come and wipe away every tear, right every wrong, and heal every malady, but until then...

until then, His grace is sufficient to carry you through every heartache, every pain, every failure, every financial lack, every loss, and every severed relationship.

During one of Chloe's many restless nights where she cried in pain in my arms until dawn broke, the Lord whispered to me, "Your breakthrough is in your praise."

I understood what He meant, but it was still hard to put His words into practice. It's easy to praise God when you receive a promotion, a raise, a new house, a better job, or a boost in your health. But the real test of our praise comes during trials and challenging times.

Paul and Silas had already been stripped and beaten for casting a demon out of a fortune teller. But it's their attitude of praise, not their suffering, that takes center stage in Acts 16:25: "About midnight Paul and Silas were praying and singing hymns to God, and the other prisoners were listening to them."

Their response to adversity was to pray and sing praises to God. They did not waste a single second on complaints, self-pity, or revenge. Instead, Paul and Silas turned pain into heartfelt prayer and sadness into joyful singing. And what happened next was astounding.

"Suddenly there was such a violent earthquake that the foundations of the prison were shaken. At once, all the prison doors flew open, and everyone's chains came loose." (Acts 16:26) Their praise unleashed their breakthrough. And their chains were not the only ones that came off that night. Every single prisoner saw chains fall off their hands and feet, too. When we pray and praise God in difficult times, God sends a breakthrough that impacts us and brings freedom to those around us as well.

"Your breakthrough is in your praise"— God's words reverberated in my spirit. I shared them with my wife and kids, and we decided that, from then on, we would turn every complaint into praise. No matter

Your breakthrough is in your praise.

how concerned we were or how bleak the situation looked, we would praise God through all our uncertainty and sorrow.

And finally, the breakthrough came. Not in the form of complete healing for Chloe yet, but in a change of perspective. As we praised God in the middle of Chloe's deteriorating health and ensuing sleepless nights, we became keenly aware of His presence, His comfort, His blessings, and His purpose.

We weren't in denial as much as we were grateful for the small victories and miracles we saw along the way. Chloe was sick, but God was still on His throne, and that made all the difference. We decided to turn our pain into purpose.

The Bible portrays Jesus as a Man of Sorrows who is acquainted with grief (Isaiah 53:5). He connects with us and comforts us in our pain and heartache. The Apostle Paul wrote in Philippians 3:10 that he learned *the fellowship of Christ's sufferings.*

Jim Elliot and four other missionaries were killed in 1956 when they attempted to contact the Huaorani people in Ecuador. Heartbroken but undeterred, Jim's wife, Elisabeth, decided to stay with her ten-month-old daughter and minister to the same tribe that killed her husband.

Elisabeth Elliot had a unique perspective on pain: "I am not a theologian or a scholar, but I am very aware of the fact that pain is necessary to all of us. In my own life, I think I can honestly say that out of the deepest pain has come the strongest conviction of the presence of God and the love of God."[8]

As C. S. Lewis wrote many years ago, "God whispers to us in our pleasures, speaks in our conscience, but shouts in our pains: It is his megaphone to rouse a deaf world."[9] We could hear God loud and clear—He was using our daughter's sickness to capture our attention.

We learned to face the pain and disappointment of unanswered prayer with honesty and courage. We discovered that sometimes God heals and other times He doesn't heal as much as He comes and stands with us in our pain and helps us carry our brokenness. We decided to love God through our pain and hurt, through our fear and doubt.

Fast forward to June 14, 2016, two months after Chloe first became ill. I hosted a breakfast for 143 local pastors and leaders with my friend, New Mexico Lieutenant Governor John Sanchez, who shared about his faith in Christ. After breakfast, I struck up a conversation with John Robb, the Chairman of the International Prayer Council.

"Have you heard of Jason Hubbard in Bellingham, Washington?" John asked.

I hadn't, and I said as much. John grinned.

"Jason has a simple model to cover Bellingham in prayer— he asks different churches in the city to adopt a monthly day of prayer. Different denominations, cultures, ages, and races unite in prayer one day at a time. I believe this is a strategy that can transform New Mexico."

I looked at John incredulously.

"You're kidding? My friend Trey Kent is doing the same thing in Austin, Texas. I couldn't agree more. Imagine the change in this city if the Lord calls someone to lead a similar movement here."

If God had revealed the vision of 24/7 prayer to John as well, I secretly hoped John would spearhead the idea himself. But no such luck.

John smiled broader and clasped my shoulder.

"I couldn't agree more. And you know what, Brian? I believe you're the man to lead it."

I felt my stomach drop.

"John, I would love to, but there's no way I can. I'm the Lead Pastor of Passion Church and work full-time for the Billy Graham Evangelistic Association. I'm out of state over twenty-five weeks a year. I have three young children, and my oldest is sick. I can't take on anything else. But I can help you if you lead it."

John held my gaze, unswayed.

"I told you, Brian. I think you're the one. But why don't you pray about it and see what the Lord tells you."

I had been praying for a long time, and God had already told me what to do. "Brian, start 24/7 prayer in every city, every state, and every nation."

A few months before this, in my capacity as a regional manager for the Billy Graham Evangelistic Association, I had traveled to Austin to help prepare for Franklin Graham's Decision America Tour prayer rally at the state capitol.

Our local coordinator for the event was Trey Kent, Pastor of Northwest Fellowship in Austin. In his book *City of Prayer,* Trey tells the story of how God inspired him to rally churches in Austin to adopt a monthly day of prayer. Trey Kent and Jason

Hubbard started their movements of unceasing prayer the same month, January 2009, eight years before they met.

In both their models, every church adopts a day or half-day of prayer once a month. Members sign up to pray for 30-60 minutes from home, work, school, church, or anywhere. Thirty-one churches committed to praying one day a month is all it takes to cover a city in 24/7 prayer.

The same model works for states and nations. You can cover your state or country in 24/7 prayer with just thirty-one churches adopting a monthly day of prayer. Once you have every day and every hour covered by at least one church, you can have multiple churches per day.

Trey and Jason didn't know each other, but Jesus was about to connect the three of us for something extraordinary. My conversation with John Robb was God's way of bringing the pieces together. Austin. Bellingham. Albuquerque. If three cities could pray independently, what would happen if we came together to seek God's face?

On June 21, 2016, I delivered the hardest Father's Day sermon of my life. I was confident in the Father's love but was struggling to understand why He hadn't healed Chloe. After all, hadn't I agreed to follow Him in the quest for 24/7 prayer coverage?

When I got home, Chloe's pain intensified. She doubled over with a sharp gasp, dropped her fork, and screamed at our Father's Day family lunch. I rushed to my daughter's side, scooped her up in my arms, and carried her to her room. When her screams subsided and she lay in a restless sleep, I turned my eyes to heaven.

Lord, why?

For a long time, that's all I could ask.

My daughter has been isolated and in pain for over two months! I love you, Lord, but I don't understand. You could heal Chloe with a single word. So, why don't you?

But again, God answered with stillness.

Thoughts flashed through my mind: *If prayer doesn't change the outcome, then why do we even bother to pray?*

And with that question, God began to open my eyes.

Often, we read Scriptures like John 14:13 and Matthew 7:7 and conclude that the point of prayer is to receive answers to our petitions. But what if we've missed the whole point? What if we, as the body of Christ at large, have lost sight of the real purpose of prayer?

In Matthew 26, Mark 14, and Luke 22, we read about what transpired before Jesus was taken into Roman custody. As the night grows dark, Jesus leads His disciples into the Garden of Gethsemane.

"Remain here while I go to pray," Jesus says. When He's all alone, He collapses to His knees.

"Father," Jesus groans, "if there is any way this cup might pass other than for me to drink it, please remove it from me. Please, Father! But if there is no other way, then let not mine, but your will be done."

And yet, the will of God doesn't relent. So, Jesus prays again.

"Father, I ask that you remove this cup from me! But if there is no other way, let your will be done."

But God's will remains the same. And Jesus prays a third time as His sweat glands bleed with crimson blood.

"Father, let your will be done, not mine."

What do you think? Did Jesus pray the wrong prayer? Did He not have enough faith to receive what He asked for?

Or was Jesus praying for a purpose far greater than what we see on the surface? What if His prayer was less about getting the answer He wanted and more about His need to surrender?

That's what God began to teach me: Prayer is so much more than requests and petitions—it's an act of surrendering our will to God's will.

PRAYER IS SURRENDER.

Prayer is an act of surrendering your will to God's will.

And so, as the summer of '16 dragged on, Mercy and I fought for a different perspective. Like Jesus in the garden, we prayed as much to know God's heart as to plead for our daughter's healing. And we committed that, regardless of the outcome, we would surrender to His will for our lives and hers.

Three months after Chloe left the hospital, Mercy and I stood in a clinic, listening to yet another doctor discuss Chloe's condition. As her stomach pain worsened, my hope began to wear thin.

"You've seen how many doctors? And you're telling me none of them figured this out?" the new doctor asked.

"No, none of them could figure it out," I conceded.

The doctor shook his head.

"Well, she's suffering from severe food allergies. Keep her away from gluten, yeast, dairy, eggs, every type of pepper, lettuce, kale…"

The list went on and on. We started Chloe on an organic treatment of distilled aloe vera, vitamins, minerals, and natural supplements. Over the coming weeks, she began to improve.

On September 23, 2016, God's nudgings to start a prayer movement became hard to ignore. Pastor Poncho Murguia from Juarez, Mexico, was set to speak at our quarterly pastors' breakfast. His story was impossible but true. In 2010, Juarez had 3,116 homicides, making it the murder capital of the world.[10] Troubled by the statistics, Poncho decided to unite various churches to pray for God to save their city.

In 2011, the number of murders in Juarez dropped to 2,086 and continued to decrease in 2012, 2013, and 2014. And then, in 2015, the number plummeted to 311.[11] Juarez had a 90 percent decrease in murders in only five years.

Later that day, I went with Poncho and several other leaders to the foothills of the Sandia Mountains to pray over Albuquerque. Afterward, Poncho pulled me aside.

"Brian, God has called you to unite your state in prayer. So, tell me, what are you waiting for?"

I sighed and responded with what was becoming a practiced answer.

"Poncho, you don't understand. I want to, but between pastoring, working for the Billy Graham Association, and taking care of my sick daughter, I don't know how I can take on one more thing."

"Don't you think you should surrender to Jesus and let Him figure out the details?" Poncho asked.

I didn't know how to respond.

"Brian, I'm going to lay my hands on you and pray. Then I want you to pray over New Mexico like she is an abused orphan girl you are about to adopt. Tell her you are going to love her, protect her, and fight for her."

After Poncho prayed, I opened my mouth and immense sorrow for my state overtook me.

"God, is this what you feel for this state?" I wondered. And then I knew. I wasn't merely sorrowful—God's heartbreak consumed me and became my own.

Prayer is an impartation of God's heart to your heart. Real prayer, birthed by the Spirit, moves you to weep over the things God weeps over and love the people He loves.

I had an epiphany. Prayer is so much more than a conversation with God—prayer is an impartation of God's heart to your heart. Real prayer, birthed by the Spirit, moves you to weep over the things God weeps over and love the people He loves. I prayed for over an hour, my tears puddling in the dirt at the base of the Sandia Mountains.

Eighteen years earlier, just a mile away from where I now knelt, Mercy and I had driven into Albuquerque for the first time as a couple. We cried then, too.

The Alarid family has called New Mexico home for almost 400 years. One of my forefathers was the last Governor of New Mexico as Mexican territory. I had spent a year of high school in Albuquerque. So, this should have felt like a homecoming of sorts, but it didn't. We felt like strangers in a strange land.

"Jesus, why did you send us to New Mexico? I don't want to be here," I prayed.

I heard the Holy Spirit recite Isaiah 35 inside my heart. "You will see this desert blossom like a rose. You will see the glory of the Lord in this land. Here the blind will see, the deaf will hear, and the lame will walk. There will be a highway here

26

called the Way of Holiness. Joy and gladness will overtake you in New Mexico, and sorrow will flee from you."

Then God spoke to me again. "You will see New Mexico united in prayer and experience revival."

At the time, I had no idea I someday would be back on this mountain, on my knees weeping for the city. But now, the realization hit me: The vision God was giving me now wasn't a new one, but an amplification of the original calling we received the first time we drove into Albuquerque. It went even farther back. It went back to my days in Bible college when I read the stories of great revivals through the centuries.

It went back to when I was fifteen years old, and God lassoed my heart five days before homecoming. It went back to when I gave my life to Christ at the age of four in Guatemala and even farther back to before I was born. When my mother was eight months pregnant with me, our pastor, Jack Hayford, laid his hands on her stomach and prayed over me. God's call on my life to unite His people in prayer had been in the making my entire life.

"Lord, I surrender," I said. "I'm all in. I don't know how to do it, but I'll start 24/7 prayer in New Mexico. And as you open doors in other cities, states, and nations, I'll follow you there, too."

I called Mercy on the way home.

"Baby, something happened to me in the mountains. I think everything we thought we knew about our lives; everything we've planned for ourselves, our entire future, is about to change."

I told her everything, and she was all in. That evening, we joined hands in prayer and devoted our lives to this new mission.

It was time to begin fighting for unceasing prayer. It was time to unite New Mexico, then America, and ultimately, every nation on the planet in day and night prayer. I was excited about the future—and scared out of my mind.

CHAPTER 4

YEAH, I'M A CHRISTIAN

S everal hours after I collapsed at church and had a radical encounter with God, I sat on my bed and stared at the wall.

"What happened?" I wondered.

I couldn't remember much, but as my mom later explained, I fell unconscious to the floor. Once I woke up, everything was different. Never had I felt so overcome by God. I couldn't stand, I couldn't talk, I couldn't think. All I could do was weep and pray. The Holy Spirit was doing a deep work of repentance inside me.

"Forgive me, Jesus! I'm sorry. Cleanse my heart and change me. If you give me another chance, I'll serve you with all my heart."

Again, I asked myself what happened. But as I reflected on it, I realized I knew. God had demanded my attention.

I went into my closet and retrieved my Bible from where it had sat untouched for over a year. I flopped onto my bed, opened the pages to the book of Matthew, and started reading. Hours passed as pages turned, and when I finished Matthew, I kept right on going through Mark and into Luke.

When I got to Luke 10:22, I stopped.

"All things have been committed to me by my Father. No one knows who the Son is except the Father, and no one knows who the Father is except the Son and those to whom the Son chooses to reveal Him."

I heard Jesus whisper, "I am going to reveal my Father to you."

What? After everything I had done the past two years— the partying, lustful thoughts, foul language, neglecting my relationship with God—Jesus was ready to forgive me, and on top of that, reveal the Father to me?

I was experiencing amazing grace. I was lost, but now I was found. I was blind, but now I could see. Where my sin abounded, God's grace abounded even more (Romans 5:20). No matter how hard I tried, I couldn't outrun God's grace or my mother's prayers.

As I stared at the wall, my thoughts took me back to when I was nine years old. I was asleep then, sunburned after a day at the water park when I awoke to the sound of my name.

I scanned the dark living room but saw nothing.

I got up and scouted the house like a ninja, poised to stop an intruder, or tackle my older brother if he was playing a trick on me. But my brother was asleep, and so were both my parents until I woke them up to ask if they called for me. They hadn't, and they insisted I go back to sleep.

That same night, I awoke a second time to the sound of my name and went to my mother's side again to ask if she had called me.

This time, her eyes scanned my face and then held my gaze for a long moment.

"Brian, do you remember the story in the Bible when God called Samuel in the middle of the night?" she asked as she caressed my hand.

"If you hear your name again, say, 'Speak, Lord, your servant is listening.'"

When I heard my name an hour later for the third time, I responded as my mother had instructed. As I listened in that holy moment, I heard God's voice call me to ministry in His Kingdom.

Now, years later, as I sat in my room in California with my Bible in front of me, God asked, "Do you remember the night I called you into ministry, Brian? The night I asked if you would serve me? Well, I'm calling you again. It's time."

With tears in my eyes, I sank to my knees on my bedroom floor. At that moment, homecoming no longer mattered. All that mattered was the call on my life.

"Alright, God. Here I am."

And with those words, my world changed.

I skipped school on Monday and Tuesday, unsure of what to do about my situation. I returned to school when I could avoid the inevitable no longer.

My girlfriend Susan spotted me across the hall and ran to me before the first period.

"Brian! Where have you been? You weren't here yesterday or the day before. I've called you like a dozen times. Homecoming is in two days!"

I looked at her, unsure of how to proceed.

"I, um…I can't go with you to homecoming, Susan. I'm so sorry!"

She stared at me in shock.

"What?"

"I don't feel right about it."

Susan's stare became a glare.

"What do you mean you don't feel right about it? I've already made plans. I've turned down every other guy so I can go with you. It's too late to get another date!"

I looked on, determined to stick to my guns. Susan took a deep breath and tried again.

"Listen, it's going to be so much fun. We don't have to stay at the dance long if that's what you're nervous about." She cocked a wry grin. "We can leave early. We can go back to Bryan's house, just the two of us…"

A few days before, those words would have tempted me to no end. Now, steel conviction overtook me.

"I'm sorry, Susan, but I'm not going!"

After a long pause, Susan spun on her heels and started walking away, but not before yelling one last thing over her shoulder.

"Have a nice life, jerk!"

We never talked again.

After school, I spotted my friend Bryan outside. He saw me and sprinted toward me.

"Dude! What the heck? Where have you been? I asked Susan about you in biology, and she's furious! She said you bailed on her for homecoming, and so she broke up with you."

I shrugged.

"Well, that's the gist of it."

"But why?" Bryan asked.

I eyed Bryan closely, doubtful he would understand. But I decided to tell him anyway.

"Because I'm lost, Bryan. Or I was. I'm a Christian, and I've been running from God for a long time. He got ahold of me on Sunday. If I'm going to stop running, it has to be now. Not next month. Not next week. Now. I'm choosing to follow Jesus again, and the way I've been living doesn't match up with how He lived."

Bryan sighed.

"Dude, I get it. You're trying to do what's right. But listen, I'm a Christian, too, and I've thought through this before. What it comes down to is…"

"What? You're a Christian?" I interrupted.

Bryan squinted like it was obvious, and I should have known all along.

"Yeah, I'm a Christian. I go to church with my parents every Sunday morning like the rest of America. And dude, I'm telling you…"

Bryan leaned in and dropped his voice, "…premarital sex is fine! Rape? Now, that's messed up. But consensual sex is fine as long as you're safe about it."

I looked into Bryan's eyes and saw this scary belief that going to church makes you saved no matter what you do. While Bryan pulled away grinning, I regained my voice.

"You're kidding, right? Have you ever read the Bible?" I asked.

Bryan looked offended.

"Dude, it's just common sense. Think about it."

That night, I replayed our conversation in my head, and one thing Bryan said in particular: "Yeah, I'm a Christian. I go to church with my parents every Sunday, like the rest of America."

Do Americans think the only thing they need to follow Jesus is to show up for church for an hour once a week?

I hadn't been following Jesus with my whole heart either for the past few years, but, unlike Bryan, I knew it.

Growing up as a child of missionaries, my parents taught me many things, and among them was that being a follower of Jesus isn't a label you claim; it's the person you become. Being a Christ-follower isn't about going to church, lifting your hands in worship, quoting Bible verses, or any other religious activity—it's about who you are on the inside.

Are you becoming more like Jesus in the way you think, speak, act, and treat people? Is Jesus changing you from the inside-out so that you reflect His love, grace, and purity?

"If America is asleep, can she be woken up?" I wondered. The question came from nowhere, but I pondered it. I was fascinated by it. And I decided to ask for a stake in the mission.

"God, please allow me to be part of arousing this nation from its slumber. I want to see the day when America is on fire for you. Let me be part of the greatest revival in history!"

CHAPTER 5

KILL YOUR OX

"**H**ey, Richard! So, I've got this crazy idea, man. What if we started an unceasing prayer movement here in New Mexico?"

It was the week after my surrender at the base of the Sandia Mountains with Poncho, and I was on the phone with my friend, Richard Mansfield, the Senior Pastor of New Beginnings Church in Albuquerque.

"Well, yeah, dude! Like a prayer vigil? We already do those around here!" Richard's voice came back through the phone, obviously trying to understand what I was asking of him.

I smiled to myself. Here goes nothing.

"No, not a prayer vigil. Let's pray twenty-four hours a day, seven days a week, 365 days a year."

"What! The whole year?" Richard blurted.

"Yeah, and not only 2017, but until Jesus comes back, whether that's in a year or a thousand years."

Richard coughed and chuckled, not in a condescending way, but disbelief.

"Brian, how are we going to do that? Are you nuts, dude?"

"No, listen," I explained. "If we get each church to commit to pray one day a month, with thirty-one churches, we can cover the whole month in prayer. What if the church were a house of prayer as Jesus prayed we would be?"

I paused to let Richard respond, and when he did, his tone had changed from unsure to amazed.

"Brian, you're crazy. And you know what? I love it! This is going to be amazing. I'm all in."

Richard and I talked for several hours about how to unite churches in prayer all over New Mexico. And we talked about spiritual awakening. After all, while prayer was our mission, our ultimate goal was a spiritual awakening.

We launched New Mexico Prays on January 1, 2017, with five churches: Passion Church, the church I pastored, Pastor Richard Mansfield and New Beginnings Church, Bishop David Cooper and New Hope Full Gospel Baptist Church, Pastor Danny Sanchez and Victory Outreach Albuquerque, and John Robb and Heights Cumberland Presbyterian.

A few weeks later, we hosted a pastors' breakfast and invited Trey Kent to come and share what God was doing in Austin through unceasing prayer. By the end of the day, five churches became forty-two. Several weeks later, Calvary Church with Skip Heitzig, the largest church in our state, joined. Calvary marked church number fifty.

Two months later, my friend Archbishop John Wester asked if he could offer New Mexico Prays to the Catholic churches in his Archdiocese. Since we agreed on the Apostles' Creed, which was our theological baseline, it was a no-brainer. This was a historic opportunity in New Mexico for Catholics and Protestants to unite in prayer.

And unite we did.

Southern Baptist, Pentecostal, Reformed, Presbyterian, Calvary Chapel, Charismatic, Catholic, Messianic Jews, and non-denominational churches all set aside theological differences to pray for our state. Blacks, Whites, Hispanics, Asians, and Native Americans united in prayer under the banner of Jesus Christ.

Rich suburban churches and poor inner-city churches came together in a way they hadn't before. Democrats and Republicans began to set aside their political differences to serve our community together.

"I've been in Albuquerque for thirty-eight years, and I've never seen pastors come together for anything like this. It is changing the climate," remarked New Mexico Ministry Network Pastor Mike Dickenson. And he spoke the truth.

As I saw God begin using prayer to heal the division between His people, I learned that only a united church can heal a divided nation.

Only a united church can heal a divided nation.

Nate Heitzig, the Executive Pastor at Calvary Church, made this powerful statement: "I've always been passionate about church unity because the reality is we're better together than we are separate. And one incredible thing about prayer is that it unites."

The amazing thing is that the seed of New Mexico Prays was sown twenty-three years before it was birthed. My friends, Pastor Jack Webb and Pastor Steve Williams, started a pastors' prayer group in Albuquerque in 1994. I had the privilege of serving on Jack's church staff for a few years and got to witness firsthand his commitment to pray for revival in New Mexico.

I know that I'm reaping the harvest of seeds others have sown for many years. We all stand on the shoulders of those who came before us. As the saying goes, *If you ever see a turtle on top of a fence post, you know he didn't get there by himself.*

We hosted the Albuquerque National Day of Prayer on May 4, 2017. The year before, about 80 people turned up for the city event. This year, over 1,500 came to Civic Plaza to pray together.

What made the difference? Now there was a network of churches praying together 24/7, so it was much easier to gather people for a corporate prayer event. Daily prayer fuels large prayer gatherings.

The rhythm of prayer we adopted is based on the National Prayer Accord, developed by Jonathan Edwards during the First Great Awakening. Edwards encouraged weekly, monthly, quarterly, and annual prayer.[12]

We encouraged churches to have a weekly prayer meeting, adopt a monthly day of prayer, connect with other pastors and churches once a quarter for prayer, fellowship, and inspiration, and gather for united prayer annually on the National Day of Prayer.

Spring soon turned to summer, and as the summer grew hotter, so did the fire of prayer throughout New Mexico. What we were doing in our city caught the attention of faith leaders in other states and cities as well.

"We just began to blow up, and it blew our minds. We discovered that pastors wanted to be part of something bigger than them, something that was so powerful," testifies Bishop David Cooper, the President of the Albuquerque African American Ministerial Alliance.

Before long, it was common for pastors and leaders in other states to tell me, "Brian, when you are ready to take 24/7 prayer national, count us in." After fasting and praying for clarity for several weeks, I felt pretty sure God was leading us to do just that.

"Honey, what would you say if I told you I think God is leading us to take New Mexico Prays to the next level? To start America Prays?" I asked Mercy one day.

She looked up at me from where she was working at the dining room table.

"I'd say, it's about time. It's what God has been putting on our hearts since the beginning, isn't it?"

In the days that followed, Mercy and I would leave our kids with my mom and go out for afternoon coffee shop dates to write the vision, mission, values, dream, and strategy of America Prays. We felt like teenagers sneaking off after school to work on our secret treehouse.

We started dreaming with our friends Ed and Elizabeth Horne about taking 24/7 prayer to every city and state in America. In July, Ed and Elizabeth invited me to Austin to flesh out the idea in its entirety.

My best friend, Bruno Interlandi, and Trey Kent joined us in person, and Mercy, Jason Hubbard, and Lewis Hogan joined through video conference. Mike Hollister led us through a step-by-step strategic planning process. America Prays was born by the end of the day. Not long afterward, my friend Dave Butts, the Chairman of the National Prayer Committee, joined our Board of Directors.

The Lord gave us the vision to unite and equip 40,000 churches in 24/7 prayer for a national spiritual awakening.

The more we prayed, the Lord expanded our vision to include individuals, families, ministries, businesses, prisons, and schools. We knew we wanted to help people everywhere pray more effectively.

As Jason Hubbard says, "We want to create canopies of united, strategic, sustainable prayer over every city, state, and nation in the world." Unceasing prayer helps create an awareness of God's presence in a community and increased receptivity to the Gospel.

THE FIRE MUST NEVER GO OUT

Praying for a day, a month, or a year is manageable. But how do you sustain prayer until Jesus returns?

As 24/7 prayer was beginning to gain traction, that was the question heavy on my heart. I don't want to give my life to something that doesn't have staying power.

Once again, I found my answer in the Scriptures, this time in Leviticus 6:9-13, "These are the regulations for the burnt offering: The burnt offering is to remain on the altar hearth throughout the night, till morning, and the fire must be kept burning on the altar. The priest shall then put on his linen clothes, with linen undergarments next to his body, and shall remove the ashes of the burnt offering that the fire has consumed on the altar and place them beside the altar.

Then he is to take off these clothes and put on others and carry the ashes outside the camp to a place that is ceremonially clean. The fire on the altar must be kept burning; the fire must never go out. Every morning the priest is to add firewood and arrange the burnt offering on the fire and burn the fat of the fellowship offerings on it.

The fire must be kept burning on the altar continuously; the fire must never go out."

This is one of the foundational Biblical passages of America Prays. What I love about Leviticus 6 is that the fire didn't sustain itself.

It was the job of the priests to go in the morning and put more firewood on the altar. They had to stoke the fire and remove the ashes from the wood that burned all night. And again at night, they had put more firewood on the altar so it would burn all night.

Sustaining the fire required organization, preparation, resources, personnel, hard work, systems, and devoted leadership. Moses needed staff to cut down the trees, chop them into firewood, haul the wood to the Tabernacle, place it on the altar, remove the ashes, and do it all over again and again.

There was a plan, structure, and system in place to keep the fire burning 24/7 in the Tabernacle of Moses, which was "the church in the wilderness" (Acts 7:38). In the same way, God wants the fire of prayer to burn continually in every heart, every home, every church, and every nation.

God was giving us a model and structure that would help individuals, families, churches, businesses, cities, states, and nations keep the fire of 24/7 prayer alive for years to come. I could see it with my spiritual eyes. Now it was time to do it.

With both New Mexico Prays and now America Prays underway, I felt led to step away from the Billy Graham Evangelistic Association. Talk about being scared! I was leaving an established organization without a guaranteed salary. That wasn't the only thing I had to let go of. For the past eleven years of my life, I had been the Lead Pastor at Passion Church. I knew it was time to start the transition from Lead Pastor to Founding Pastor.

I remember saying to God, "Passion Church is my baby. I love this church. Do I have to give her up?"

Jesus' response brought me to my knees.

"Will you sacrifice your baby for my church and devote the rest of your life to help my bride get closer to me in prayer?"

I was scared to step away from two anchors I knew so well, but I was also excited. I knew that while our plans may offer us a feeling of security, God's plans provide a far greater adventure.

Like H. Jackson Brown wrote in his book, *P.S. I Love You*: "Twenty years from now you will be more disappointed by the things that you didn't do than by the ones you did do. So, throw off the bowlines. Sail away from the safe harbor. Catch the trade winds in your sails."[13]

You are the most secure when you surrender everything to Jesus and lay down your life, your dreams, and your ambitions at the foot of the cross.

I was putting away my security blanket with Passion Church and the Billy Graham Evangelistic Association, and right then, Jesus taught me a valuable lesson—you are the most secure when you are the most vulnerable.

I love the radical challenge Jesus issued in Matthew 16:24-26: "Anyone who intends to come with me has to let me lead. You're not in the driver's seat; I am. Don't run from suffering; embrace it. Follow me, and I'll show you how. Self-help is no help at all. Self-sacrifice is the way, my way, to finding yourself, your true self. What kind of deal is it to get everything you want but lose yourself? What could you ever trade your soul for?"[14]

When Elisha received his call to serve God, he wanted to be fully committed. He didn't want to have a backup plan. So, he slaughtered his oxen and used the wood from the yokes to burn their flesh (1 Kings 19:21).

This represented his whole livelihood. If you owned a restaurant, it would be like burning it to the ground and firing all your employees. Elisha was hardcore. And as Jack Black once said, "You're not hardcore unless you live hardcore."[15]

But nobody in history was more hardcore than Jesus.

Jesus declared in Luke 9:23-24: "If anyone wants to come after Me, he must deny himself and take up his cross daily and follow Me. For whoever wants to save his life will lose it, but whoever loses his life for My sake will save it."

In layman's terms, Jesus is saying, "Look, if you want to follow Me and be My disciple, you have to die to your dreams, your selfish ambitions, and your sinful lifestyle. Take up your cross every single day, choose My will over your will, and follow Me."

In 1873, Evangelist Dwight L. Moody visited Dublin, Ireland, and met a British revivalist named Henry Varley. He looked Moody right in the eyes and challenged him, "Moody, the world has yet to see what God will do with a man fully consecrated to him."[16]

These words had a profound impact on Moody and motivated him for the rest of his life. God is calling you to be fully devoted to Him. Jesus unapologetically demands to be first in your life. Will you respond to Him?

Discipleship is an invitation to die to yourself and live only for Jesus.

Discipleship is an invitation to die to yourself and live only for Jesus. As my friend Pastor Josh White once told me in Portland, "Christianity is not a ladder to climb, but a cross we die on."

I memorized Galatians 2:20 when I was a boy, and it still convicts and challenges me today. "I have been crucified with Christ, and I no longer live, but Christ lives in me. The life I now live in the body, I live by faith in the Son of God, who loved me and gave himself for me."

George Müller was a 19th-century minister who pastored the same church for over sixty-six years in Bristol, England. He cared for over 10,000 orphans during his lifetime and established 117 schools that provided Christian education to more than 120,000 children.

What was the secret to his success and longevity in ministry? Müller testified: "There was a day when I died, utterly died, to George Müller, his opinions, preferences, tastes, and will—died to the world, its approval or censure—died to the approval or blame of even my brethren and friends—and since then I have studied to show myself approved only unto God."[17]

Jesus articulated it this way in John 12:24, "I tell you the truth, unless a kernel of wheat is planted in the soil and dies, it remains alone. But its death will produce many new kernels—a plentiful harvest of new lives."[18] When you are willing to die to yourself, that death produces resurrection, life, and fruitfulness.

John the Baptist proclaimed in John 3:30, "He must increase, but I must decrease."[19] To the degree you are willing to decrease, to that same degree, Christ can increase in your life. Are you willing to die to your pride, ego, and selfish ambitions and live for the glory of God?

Are you willing to let go of the comfortable and embrace the uncertainty of the cross?

Will you embrace the reality of the crucified life and forsake everything to pursue the nail-scarred Rabbi from Nazareth?

Are you ready to kill your ox and follow Jesus?

CHAPTER 6

ON THE CORNER OF FULTON AND WILLIAM STREETS

Two more years of high school followed after I rededicated my life to Christ. Then, with a bang, high school was over, and I was seventeen years old.

I was hungry for God and desperate to experience Him move in my personal life and my generation. Attending Bible college in Upstate New York felt like the right next step. A friend bought me a one-way ticket to New York, and my college adventure began in January 1992.

"Hey, man! What's your name?"

I turned to see a built, handsome student walking toward me right before the first lecture of the day. I swapped my armful of notebooks to my left arm and extended my right hand.

"Hey! I'm Brian."

The student shook my hand. "Good to meet you! I'm Lance. Are you new on campus?"

I nodded.

"Don't worry; you're welcome to sit by me if you like."

From that point on, Lance and I became the best of friends. (Sometimes we would even go down to the garage and do karate together.) We joined an early morning prayer meeting and spent hundreds of hours praying for revival over the next few years.

We both burned for revival in our nation, and as far as we knew, renowned Christian leader Dr. A. T. Pierson had it right when he asserted, "There has never been a spiritual awakening in any country or locality that did not begin in united prayer."[20] The words of author Leonard Ravenhill also motivated me to pursue God: "No man is greater than his prayer life."[21]

> *There has never been a spiritual awakening in any country or locality that did not begin in united prayer.*
>
> —*Dr. A. T. Pierson*

When you study Scripture and church history, you discover the two critical components of every revival and awakening that made a lasting impact are prayer and the Word of God. Prayer is often the spark that ignites revival in a person, community, or church, but without God's Word, it's impossible to experience sustained life change. The early apostles devoted themselves to prayer and God's Word above everything else (Acts 6:4).

The most significant revival in the Old Testament occurred when the Scriptures were discovered after years of being lost. King Josiah wept when he heard God's Word read, and it changed his heart and awakened the consciousness of a nation. The public reading of Scripture brought conviction and led to a mass rejection of idolatry, immorality, and wickedness.

Nehemiah chapters 8 and 9 chronicle the revival that took place when Ezra, the priest of Israel, stood before the people in the Jerusalem square and "read from the book of the Law."

As my friend Morgan Jackson says, "The greatest revival in history came from hearing God's Word when Jesus came, and the Father said, 'This is my beloved son: listen to Him.'"

The importance of God's word to genuine revival cannot be overstated. When prayer accompanies the Scriptures, it is a powerful combination that can lead to personal and corporate revival, life change, and societal transformation.

> *When prayer accompanies the Scriptures, it is a powerful combination that can lead to personal and corporate revival, life change, and societal transformation.*

One Friday night, Lance and I were at a chapel service. The guest speaker was in the heat of his message when he paused, without warning, looked at me for a long moment, and then called me forward.

I followed my orders.

"What's your name, young man?" The speaker asked.

I told him.

"God has impressed on my heart that He has called you to be an intercessor who prays for revival. You want to be a great preacher, I can tell. But prayer is your first calling."

"Your prayer life is your covenant with God, like Samson's hair. If you guard your prayer life and let it continue to grow, God's anointing on you will continue to increase."

I swallowed to keep my jaw from dropping.

Those words penetrated the deepest recesses of my heart, and I found it impossible to dismiss them. They were stuck in my head. Moved by the speaker, I spent the whole night in prayer with Lance and a few other classmates.

Around 2 a.m., God's still, small voice brushed my heart.

"Brian, what do you think would happen if you spent eight hours in prayer every day for a whole year?"

I blinked. Eight hours of prayer a day. *Say what?*

"God, I would love to do that, but I mean, I have class and homework and work duties and laundry. And I have to eat and sleep at some point."

"Brian, I love you, and I want to spend time with you. I want you to know my heart, and I want to teach you my Word. What do you say?"

It wasn't a command or a directive—it was more like a gentle invitation into a deeper level of prayer and intimacy than I had never even imagined.

"I want to, Lord, but I have no idea how to do that."

The invitation remained. After a pause, I reconsidered.

"But, if you will teach me, I'll sure try."

And teach me He did.

I started to pray constantly—not always in solitude, but in step with the rest of life. I prayed while I was doing laundry, washing dishes, studying, writing term papers, and even playing ping pong, volleyball, or card games with friends. I learned how to practice the presence of God.

God began to teach me that prayer doesn't always have to be something we set aside time to do—it can be the way we live every second of every day. The Holy Spirit taught me how to cultivate His presence in everything I did, big and small. Praying and living in God's presence moved from being a separate activity to a way of life as Jesus modeled. He prayed with as much conviction in the middle of dinner conversations (John 12:27-28) as He did in solitude on mountain tops (Luke 6:12).

Jesus is the greatest intercessor in history. To become like Jesus is to become a person of prayer. Jesus' prayer life made the biggest impact on His disciples, which explains why they asked Jesus to teach them how to pray (Luke 11:1).

If I had been there, I might have asked Jesus to teach me how to turn water into wine, preach, or heal the sick. But the disciples recognized what many of us miss: Jesus' devotion to prayer was His special connection to the Father that released supernatural power on His ministry.

I love the way my friend Pete Greig expresses it: "The greatest person who ever lived was preeminently a man of prayer. Before launching out in public ministry, He fasted for more than a month in the wilderness. Before choosing His twelve disciples, He prayed all night."[22]

> *Jesus' devotion to prayer was His special connection to the Father that released supernatural power on His ministry.*

PRAYER IS INTIMACY

The primary purpose of prayer is intimacy with God. Jesus longs to have an intimate relationship with you, and prayer is one of the primary ways you can connect with Him.

Before you ask God for anything in prayer, spend time with Him in fellowship. When the disciples asked Jesus to teach them how to pray, He instructed them to start with relationship: "Our Father in heaven."

PRAYER IS INTIMACY.

The primary purpose of prayer is intimacy with God.

We have access to God's throne room because of our relationship as His children. As Manhattan pastor Timothy Keller wrote, "The only person who dares wake up a king at 3:00 a.m. for a glass of water is a child. We have that kind of access."[23]

King David exemplified this hunger for intimacy with God in Psalm 27:4, "One thing I ask from the Lord, this only do I seek: that I may dwell in the house of the Lord all the days of my life, to gaze on the beauty of the Lord and to seek Him in His temple." And in Exodus 33:11, God considers Moses not only His servant but also His friend. "The Lord would speak to Moses face to face, as a man speaks with his friend."

Why settle for a superficial relationship with Jesus when you can have an intimate, face-to-face friendship with Him? Jesus is impartial—He loves all His children equally. But while He doesn't have *favorites*, He does have *intimate friends*, meaning He is more intimate with some of His children than He is with others. The great thing is that you can be as close to God as you want to be.

Intimacy with Christ is not reserved for the elite but the hungry. *Are you hungry for God?*

AWAKENING

The next semester, one of my professors assigned a unique reading project: The life of Count Nikolaus Ludwig, Reichsgraf von Zinzendorf und Pottendorf. (Yes, that's one name with a comma in the middle.)

I suppose most students would have balked, but I couldn't wait to get started. I'm nerdy like that.

The story is this. Zinzendorf was born in Dresden, Germany, on May 26, 1700. He was heir to the fortune of one of Europe's leading families.

Even as a young child, Zinzendorf had a special touch from God. When he was six years old, Swedish soldiers broke into the castle where he lived. They were so amazed to hear the young boy praying to God so passionately they spared his life.

When he was a young man, Zinzendorf had an encounter with God while he was looking at a painting of Christ wearing the crown of thorns. There was an inscription that read, "I have done this for you; what have you done for me?"

Deeply moved, Zinzendorf said, "I have loved Christ for a long time, but I have never actually done anything for Him. From now on I will do whatever He leads me to do."

Beginning in 1722, Zinzendorf began taking in immigrants to live on his vast estate. His small community was called Herrnhut, which means "The Lord's watch."

On August 5, 1727, Zinzendorf and fourteen others spent the entire night in prayer, seeking the presence of God. Eight days later, they experienced a mighty outpouring of the Holy Spirit as a deep conviction of sin fell upon the community.

Two weeks later, Zinzendorf organized a prayer chain with at least two people praying every hour of the day, 24 hours a day. This prayer meeting continued for over a century!

This Moravian community prayed 24 hours a day for over 100 years straight, but they didn't just pray. Through unceasing prayer, their hearts became consumed with a burden and a passion for people far from God. By the time Zinzendorf died in 1760, the Moravian community had sent out 226 missionaries.[24]

Several of these Moravians developed such a burden for the lost that they were even willing to sell themselves into slavery so they could lead slaves to Christ. Their love for Jesus was the driving force behind their passion for reaching the lost. The Moravians had a saying that exemplified their devotion to Jesus: "May the Lamb that was slain receive the reward of His suffering." These Moravians gave birth to the modern missions movement. Prayer and reaching people far from God are always intricately connected. When you commune with God through prayer, He gives you His heart for the lost.

When I read the story of Zinzendorf, I remembered what God asked me when He first suggested the idea of unceasing prayer: "Brian, what do you think would happen if you prayed eight hours every day for a whole year?" Now I knew.

I wrote in my journal, "Lord, let me be part of a modern-day Moravian prayer movement."

> *Prayer is the womb of revival. Every awakening in history was birthed in prayer.*

I thought to myself: *Prayer is the womb of revival. Every awakening in history was birthed in prayer. And if prayer is what brings revival, then I want to learn everything I can about prayer.*

But my training in prayer was just beginning.

Another book I read back in those days had to do with Jonathan Edwards. To tell his story, let me take you back to Colonial America in the early 1700s.

At that time, Christianity was well established in America as the primary religion, but spiritual fervor and passion for God were at an all-time low. Before the fires of Revolution swept

across the nation, another type of fire spread across America—
revival fire. Revival broke out in Northampton, Massachusetts
in 1734 and 1735 in the church of Pastor Jonathan Edwards.

This was the beginning of the First Great Awakening that
radically transformed colonial America and England.

Some pastors criticized Edwards' revival as nothing more
than spiritual emotionalism and fanaticism. People who had
been overcome by the conviction of sin at Edwards' services
would run around, cry, shout, and roll around on the floor.
Under harsh criticism from other religious leaders, the revival
began to dissipate in 1735 and waned for several years.

In 1739, George Whitefield came to America and began
preaching all over New England. He preached to open-air
crowds of 20,000 people.

Whitefield made a stop in Massachusetts in 1740. He met
with Edwards' congregation and reminded them of the revival
they had experienced only a few years before. He encouraged
them to pray and seek God for revival again.

Edwards was touched by the Holy Spirit and wept through
the whole service. That day brought a new wave of praying for
revival at his church, and Jonathan Edwards began traveling
and calling people to repentance.

On July 8, 1741, in Enfield, Connecticut, Jonathan Edwards
preached his famous sermon, *Sinners in the Hands of an Angry
God.* He gave eleven reasons why God is justified in sending
people to hell if they don't repent. As he spoke, the spirit of
conviction began to fall upon the church.

Witnesses who were there testified that people began to
moan and groan under the weight of conviction. People fell
to the ground and started crying as he was preaching. This

sparked the next great wave of revival in America. Meanwhile, in England, John and Charles Wesley were leading tens of thousands of people to Christ with a similar call to repentance.

As the semester continued, I also read the story of the New York City noon prayer meeting that sparked another wave of revival.

A businessman named Jeremiah Lanphier accepted an offer to be the community missionary for the North Dutch Church in Lower Manhattan in the summer of 1857. The Lord impressed on him to start a weekly prayer meeting. He printed and distributed 20,000 flyers across New York City.

On Wednesday, September 23, 1857, Jeremiah waited in anticipation for crowds of people to show up for his noontime prayer meeting, but nobody showed up. He was discouraged but kept praying. At 12:30 p.m., the first guest arrived and then another and another until six people joined him in prayer for the last thirty minutes.

It wasn't what he had hoped for, but it was a start. As Zechariah 4:10 says, "Do not despise the day of small beginnings."

Within two weeks, his weekly prayer meeting grew to forty people, and Jeremiah decided to make it a daily prayer gathering. On October 14, the stock market crashed, and the prayer meeting exploded. Within six months, 10,000 people (mostly businessmen) were gathering every day for prayer at noon in New York City.

Who would have imagined that this little prayer meeting, on the corner of Fulton and William Streets, would be the spark of the Great Revival of 1857-1858?

This movement then spread to other major cities—Chicago, Philadelphia, Cleveland, Louisville, and St. Louis—before sweeping across the nation. Over a million Americans dedicated their lives to Christ between 1858 and 1859, out of a population of 31 million.

This wasn't a church revival—it was a marketplace revival. It was known as the Layman's Prayer Revival because business people led it rather than clergy.

My hunger for revival grew even more intense when I read the story of Evan Roberts, who worked in the coal mines of Wales from the age of 11 to 23. Evan was just an ordinary guy, but he had an encounter with God that transformed him.

When he was twenty-six years old, Evan felt the call of God and began to prepare for ministry. Evan was desperate for God and started waking up every morning at 1 a.m. to pray for three or four hours. This went on for several months.

One night in the fall of 1904, Evan had an encounter with God as he was praying in a garden. He went inside and told his best friend, Sydney Evans, "I had a vision of all Wales being lifted up to heaven. We are going to see the mightiest revival that Wales has ever known....Do you believe that God can give us one hundred thousand souls?"[25]

Evan and Sydney began traveling all around Wales, preaching the Gospel with several young women who sang before they preached.

Thousands of people committed their lives to Jesus, and the nation was transformed. Welsh judges were given white gloves because there were no criminal cases to try.[26] Revival wiped out crime, alcoholism was cut in half, and many taverns closed.

Within six months, over 100,000 people gave their lives to Christ.

Having heard stories from the revival, author and evangelist Frank Bartleman wrote to Evan Roberts and asked him how to bring revival to Los Angeles. Evan replied, "Congregate the people who are willing to make a total surrender. Pray and wait. Believe God's promises. Hold daily meetings. May God bless you is my earnest prayer."[27]

In April 1906, the Holy Spirit visited Los Angeles in what became known as the Azusa Street Revival. As Pastor Jim Cymbala wrote, "Prayer begets revival, which begets more prayer."

Missionary leader Andrew Murray observed, "The coming revival must begin with a great prayer revival. It is in the closet, with the door shut, that the sound of abundance of rain will be first heard. An increase of secret prayer with ministers and members will be the sure harbinger of blessing."[28]

It's been over twenty-eight years since I first read these stories, but they continue to inspire me today. The church of Jesus Christ is still in need of a genuine Biblical revival, and the world desperately needs another great awakening.

What is revival, and why is it so important that we pray for it?

The best definition of *revival* I've found comes from my friend Richard Blackaby and his father Henry, the co-authors of *Experiencing God*: "Revival is a divinely initiated work in which God's people pray, repent of their sin, and return to a holy, Spirit-filled, obedient, love-relationship with God."[29]

This is the message of 2 Chronicles 7:14: "If my people, who are called by my name, will humble themselves and pray and seek my face and turn from their wicked ways, then I will hear from heaven, and I will forgive their sin and will heal their land." Revivals often start with one or two people who get a burden for prayer.

Jonathan Edwards wrote, "God's people will be given a spirit of prayer, inspiring them to come together and pray in an extraordinary manner, that He would help His Church, show mercy to mankind in general, pour out His Spirit, revive His work, and advance His kingdom in the world as He promised. Moreover, such prayer would gradually spread and increase… ushering in a revival of religion."[30]

God used all kinds of people to ignite revival—a twenty-six-year-old coal miner in Wales, a one-eyed Black preacher in Los Angeles, and a businessman in New York City. If you get desperate for God, seek His face, humble yourself, and repent of your sins, you could be the person God uses to spark a revival in your business, school, college, church, city, or nation.

You are a revival waiting for a place to happen.

You got next!

CHAPTER 7

A NAKED DUDE AND 80,000 POUNDS OF HOPE

M y son Colin and I jumped out of the car and ran to the movie theater ticket booth.

"Two tickets for *The Greatest Showman,* please."

The ticket teller looked up at me, smacked the gum in her mouth, and then took the debit card from my outstretched hand. Minutes later, Colin and I were hunkered down in the auditorium with popcorn and Coke waiting for the previews to start.

It was January 23, 2018, and I had kept Colin home from school that morning to go with me to my legislators' Bible study at the State Capitol in Santa Fe. Afterward, I opened the New Mexico House of Representatives in prayer, took Colin on the Capitol tour, and introduced him to the elected officials I had become friends with over the years.

I know Colin has a calling on his life to minister to government leaders as I do, and I wanted to be intentional about exposing him to opportunities at a young age. Now, it was time to catch a movie. While the previews were still showing, my phone started to buzz. I looked to see who it was.

"Springfield, Missouri," the caller ID read on my phone from a number I didn't recognize. I stepped outside the theater for a moment to answer it.

"Brian! This is Doug Clay. How are you doing, man of God?"

I felt my mouth go dry. *Doug Clay?* The newly elected General Superintendent of the Assemblies of God, the largest Protestant denomination in the world with over 375,000 churches?

"Hey, Pastor Doug! How are you doing?"

"I'm good, thanks. I heard you started America Prays. Congratulations! Listen, Brian, we believe in the vision God has given you to cover America in prayer, and we want to partner with you. Would you consider coming to Houston in July to share the vision of America Prays with all our district superintendents in the U.S.?"

I was speechless. The prayer movement that started in New Mexico went national with the launch of America Prays in the past three months. In that time, God had given us a clear vision, strategy, and committed Board of Directors and Advisers. Funding was coming in slow but steady. Incredible partnerships were already forming.

Dick Eastman, the international president of Every Home for Christ, had already come on board as our Senior Adviser. That all happened in three months. Now, the Lord was opening doors for us to partner with the largest movement of churches in the world.

And God was just getting started.

In April, my friend Leslie Keegel invited Jason Hubbard and me to spend the day with him in Anaheim. Leslie is the Global Chairman of the Foursquare Church, which has over 100,000 churches around the world.

Leslie prayed over me and encouraged me: "I see you throwing a net. This net will cover every nation, the entire globe. This net will bring a firewall that will protect the church from evil and will bring revival to every nation."

Then Leslie looked me right in the eyes.

"Brian, I want our 100,000 churches to partner with you to cover every nation in 24/7 prayer. Let's do it together. We already have thousands of believers praying in Sri Lanka. Can Sri Lanka join your network today?"

With that, Sri Lanka became our first foreign country. The next week, churches in India and Japan joined the movement. Then, with the Spirit's leading, we launched World Prays to serve as our global network. And just like that, within six months of starting America Prays, this 24/7 prayer movement had already spread to many nations.

I remembered something the Lord had often told me over the years: "When I want to bless you, anything works. When I want to humble you, nothing works." It was God's time to bless us.

> *When God wants to bless you, anything works. When God wants to humble you, nothing works.*

Three months later, I forced my eyes open to slits. Darkness loomed overhead, and I was sure the time was still closer to "last night" than "this morning." I would have rolled over and fallen back asleep, but my phone buzzed. Then it buzzed again. And again.

With a frustrated grunt, I grabbed my phone from the nightstand and answered it.

"Hello?"

"Brian, you're not going to believe it." The voice of my friend, Jason Dickenson, came through.

"What?" I asked, hearing the tension in his voice.

Jason paused as if trying to determine the best way to deliver his news.

"We don't have any power at the convention center. And without electricity, the fire marshal obviously won't let us have our event."

I shook my head, trying to wake myself up.

"Wait; what?"

"Yeah, it appears someone broke in during the middle of the night and destroyed the electrical panel."

It was June 23, 2018, and over 100 churches, ministries, businesses, and government agencies had partnered with us to sponsor our first Convoy of Hope community outreach in Albuquerque. Jason and I co-chaired this event together.

An hour later, I arrived at the Albuquerque Convention Center to inspect the damage. Not that I was any help. Sure enough, much of the electrical wiring in the convention center was torn apart and scrambled.

On the security camera footage, the police watched a guy break into the convention center, stumble back up to his bare feet, and take off running down the hall in his birthday suit. He passed vending machines packed with food and, instead of breaking into those, he chose the locked door of the electrical room. He was naked and on a mission to take out the power, for reasons nobody knew.

I could hear my inner Gollum saying, *Sneaky little hobbitses. Wicked, tricksy, false!*[31]

With minutes to spare, the engineers finished repairing the electrical panel and restored power to the convention center. We were back in business.

The front doors of the convention center opened around 9 a.m., and thousands of people already in line outside began flooding in. As teams of volunteers welcomed our guests, I strolled over to the VIP entrance to meet a special visitor: Tim Keller, the newly elected Mayor of Albuquerque.

"Mayor!" I called out when I spotted Tim.

Mayor Keller walked toward me, and I shook his hand.

"I'm so glad you made it today!" I said.

Mayor Keller smiled and scanned the convention center, already flooded with thousands of people.

"I'm glad I could, too. This looks incredible!" Keller said. Mayor Keller and I talked as we toured each of the offerings within the convention center. I showed him the section where mothers were helping their children try on new pairs of shoes, took him and showed him fathers collecting groceries for their families, children playing on inflatable bounce houses, and people eating lunch from Chick-fil-A. Every section and all the supplies therein were free of charge.

When Mayor Keller approached the podium to speak at our press conference, he remarked, "This is the best community outreach event I've ever attended. Let's make Convoy of Hope an annual event every year of my administration!"

When he sat down, we chatted for a few minutes.

"Brian, I meant what I said. This is the best outreach event I've been to. What do you need from me to do this again next year?" Mayor Keller asked.

"Thank you, Mayor. Would you be willing to sponsor the $38,000 rent of the convention center?"

"Absolutely. And not only that, but we can also help with marketing." A few weeks later, Mayor Keller kept his promise and sponsored the rent for our 2019 event.

By the end of the day, we had given away over $1 million worth of goods and services, including 80,000 pounds of groceries, 9,900 meals, 1,600 gardens in a bag, 3,000 pairs of shoes, and a full medical clinic from Presbyterian Healthcare.

I woke up at 3 a.m. the next morning with an intense drawing to pray. Unable to shake it, I got out of bed and knelt on the floor. And as I prayed, I began connecting the dots between Scripture and what we had done at Convoy of Hope a few hours before.

In Genesis chapter 41, we read the account of Joseph interpreting Pharaoh's dream. Joseph stands in Pharaoh's court and addresses him:

"Pharaoh, the dream foreshadows the next fourteen years. The seven good cows represent seven plentiful years, as do the seven good ears of corn; both dreams are one. The seven ravaged cows that ate the first seven represent seven years of extreme famine, and the seven diseased ears of corn also represent seven years of famine; both those dreams are one, as well."

"Now, if it pleases you, let Pharaoh appoint overseers over the land and conserve a fifth of all food produced during the next seven plentiful years and keep it in storehouses. When the seven years of famine come, your kingdom will be prepared."

Pharaoh admired Joseph's proposal, and after he consulted his advisers, he spoke to Joseph.

"I see that God has shown you all this, and therefore, there is none so discerning and wise as you. You shall be over my house, and all my people shall obey your command. Only as it regards the throne will I be greater than you."

Then, Pharaoh takes the signet ring from his finger and places it on Joseph's. "See, I have set you over all the land of Egypt. For what other man is there like you, in whom is the Spirit of God?" (Genesis 41, paraphrased)

"It isn't just Joseph who was meant to bring restoration to his nation," I thought. "No, it is the church at large."

Then, I heard the whisper of God's voice.

"The church can be to the city what Joseph was to Pharaoh and solve problems no one has been able to solve."

I meditated on what that meant. Crime, poverty, homelessness, child hunger, drug addiction—every systemic problem the city was failing at, God could solve through His people.

Christ can solve any human crisis through a united church. And nothing has the power to unite the church like prayer.

The next week, I had lunch with Mike Geier, the Albuquerque Chief of Police, to flesh out the idea with him.

"Chief, what if there was a way for the faith community to come alongside you and partner with your police department?"

Chief dunked a tortilla chip in queso sauce and nodded.

"I would want to hear about it," he replied.

I leaned in, excited.

"Convoy of Hope last weekend gave me an idea. What if God could use the church to be the solution to problems facing our city? One of those problems is crime. I believe unified prayer in this city could reduce crime rates."

I chewed on my own words for a moment, then continued.

"Chief, I want to make the Albuquerque Police Department one of our main prayer points at New Mexico Prays. I want to see you and your officers being prayed for nonstop by the churches in this city. Also, would you be open to me coming once a month to pray with you and your officers in person?"

Chief didn't answer at first. He dipped his head slightly, shook it as if to himself, then looked back up at me, his eyes already damp.

"Thank you, Brian. I agree with you. The prayers and support of the faith community in Albuquerque would help reduce crime and make our city safer. I would love to partner with you."

And so began our partnership with Chief Geier and the Albuquerque Police Department. I believed prayer would be the foundation of transformation, but we had to build an edifice of action atop our prayers. As the Bible says, faith without works is dead.

Our city and state were in a desperate place. In 2017, New Mexico was ranked No. 1 in property crime, burglary, and robbery,[32] and No. 2 in violent crime and auto theft.[33] As a city, Albuquerque ranked No. 1 in the nation in auto theft.[34] We needed a miracle in the worst possible way.

Could day and night prayer make a dent in crime? We believed it would.

We took to heart the words of the prophet in Jeremiah 29:7: "Seek the peace and prosperity of the city to which I have carried you into exile. Pray to the LORD for it because if it prospers, you too will prosper."

As we prayed and partnered with the police department, God answered our prayers in ways we never imagined. We sought God's face, and He showed us His hand.

According to the FBI, we witnessed a significant reduction in crime in Albuquerque from 2017[35] to 2018:[36]

- Robbery decreased by 32.5 percent.
- Larceny-theft decreased by 18.9 percent.
- Property crime decreased by 16.3 percent.
- Auto theft decreased by 13.9 percent.
- Burglary decreased by 8.8 percent.
- Murder decreased by 1.4 percent.

Prayer and the hard work of the Albuquerque Police Department brought about significant change. This was a modern-day illustration of unceasing prayer releasing justice on the Earth. This was Luke 18:1-8 happening in 2018.

One day Jesus told his disciples a story to show that they should always pray and never give up. "There was a judge in a certain city," he said, "who neither feared God nor cared about people. A widow of that city came to him repeatedly, saying, 'Give me justice in this dispute with my enemy.' The judge ignored her for a while, but finally he said to himself, 'I don't fear God or care about people, but this woman is driving me crazy. I'm going to see that she gets justice, because she is wearing me out with her constant requests!'"

Then the Lord said, "Learn a lesson from this unjust judge. Even he rendered a just decision in the end. So, don't you think God will surely give justice to his chosen people who cry out to him day and night? Will he keep putting them off? I tell you, he will grant justice to them quickly! But when the Son of Man returns, how many will he find on the earth who have faith?"[37]

PRAYER RELEASES JUSTICE.

Justice is heaven's response to unceasing prayer.

Jesus stated that if His chosen ones cry out to Him day and night, He will send them justice quickly. In other words, justice is heaven's response to unceasing prayer.

"New Mexico Prays is a big part of our community policing initiatives. Having people pray for us every day and for our city, I know I feel it, and I know our officers feel it," Chief Geier testified to the impact our prayer movement had on the city of Albuquerque. "And I would say to every police chief in America that you should partner with America Prays in your city."

God made it clear through the prophet Jeremiah that prayer plays a vital role in both the safety and prosperity of our communities. Prayer was helping reduce crime, but could prayer also help turn around the economy of an economically depressed state?[38]

At the beginning of 2017, New Mexico ranked 49th in economy,[39] and had the second highest poverty rate in the nation.[40] But when God's people pray, God hears from heaven, and things change. New Mexico went from a $200 million deficit[41] at the beginning of 2017 to a $1.2 billion surplus by January 2019.[42]

To be clear, new economic policies, a thriving oil and gas industry, and the hard work of many have made this possible, but this economic turnaround is too big for any politician to claim the credit. This is God working through the prayers of His people to transform the economy of a state.

Since we began unceasing prayer in New Mexico, Facebook, Netflix, and NBC Universal have brought significant jobs to our state.

Jobs are a spiritual issue. Before Adam and Eve had a house or a church or even clothes, they had a job—to take care of the Garden. They were *naked and employed*. According to Bloomberg News, New Mexico was No. 1 in job increase rate and wage increase rate in 2017.[43]

Unceasing prayer had a significant impact on reducing crime and adding jobs to our economy and transforming a $200 million deficit into a $1.2 billion surplus.

"Many people are coming into our state, saying this is the place to be. That was not the case two years ago," declared New Mexico State Representative David Gallegos. "God's changed it through prayer and allowed us to be a blessed state. And New Mexico Prays is a big part of that transformation."

Then, we saw 24/7 prayer make an impact on abortion.

Albuquerque has been known as the "late-term abortion capital of America."[44] Since churches began praying 24/7 for an end to late-term abortion in New Mexico, three abortion clinics have closed.[45]

For over two decades, the University of New Mexico Health and Sciences Department conducted research on aborted baby parts. In a remarkable turn of events, UNM has now ended that controversial program.[46]

On March 14, 2019, eight Democrat senators crossed party lines to vote for life and defeat House Bill 51.[47] It seemed impossible, but Jesus responded to the prayers of His people and moved the hearts of senators to stand for life.

Pastor Vince Torres, the Executive Director of Family Policy Alliance of New Mexico, helped lead the charge to mobilize prayer at the capitol to defeat this bill. Torres explained, "Our strategy to defeat HB 51 was to create a unified front with our local allies and mobilize pastors and churches to pray and engage."

Unceasing prayer is releasing justice on the Earth: reducing crime, transforming economies, and impacting abortion. If you want to see justice for your family, your community, and the unborn—begin crying out to God day and night.

We believe a praying church is also a compassionate church that serves the poor and neglected. Acts 1:14 reveals the early church was devoted to unceasing prayer: "These all with one mind were continually devoting themselves to prayer."

Their lifestyle of prayer gave birth to generosity and compassion, as seen in Acts 2:44-45: "All the believers were together and had everything in common. They sold property and possessions to give to anyone who had need." Both then and now, when God's people pray, He gives us His heart for the destitute.

Serving the poor is not an add-on to the Gospel—it's at the heart of the Gospel message. In His first sermon, Jesus declared in Luke 4:18, "The Spirit of the Lord is on me because He has anointed me to proclaim good news to the poor." Jesus made it clear the Gospel has a particular application for the impoverished.

James 1:27 confirms the importance of serving the poor: "Pure and undefiled religion before our God and Father is this: to care for orphans and widows in their distress."

Compassionate service to the poor confirms our message that God is love. As William Booth, the founder of the Salvation Army, once proclaimed, "You cannot warm the hearts of people with God's love if they have an empty stomach and cold feet."[48]

New Mexico Prays churches are not only uniting in prayer but also to serve our communities. We partnered with Feed New Mexico Kids and Albuquerque Public Schools to provide 2,000 needy families with Thanksgiving meals in 2018 and 3,100 families in 2019.

This prayer movement is mobilizing churches and believers to serve the destitute, and government leaders, both Republican and Democrat, are taking notice of the impact a unified church can make. That's the beautiful thing about prayer—it transcends politics, race, culture, generations, and theological differences.

> *Prayer transcends politics, race, culture, generations, and theological differences.*

"I have never seen anything like New Mexico Prays, and I have been in public office for over twenty years," Albuquerque City Councilor Ken Sanchez reflected on our partnership. "It's great to see the community rising to the challenges we are facing. The volunteerism that I have seen through New Mexico Prays is miraculous. It's amazing to see the thousands of people who are giving their time and money to help the needy in our city."

Instead of approaching government leaders asking for a donation, we come with a servant's towel to serve them and pray for them. And leaders from both political parties have partnered with us to serve the poor, feed the hungry, address homelessness, and reduce crime.

Over the past two years, Mayor Keller and I have been able to put aside our political differences and work together for the good of our city. Mayor Keller asked me to be part of his Homeless Advisory Council and also serve as a City of Albuquerque Ambassador. We have developed a genuine friendship and partnership that has impacted our city.

"It has been an absolute pleasure partnering with Pastor Alarid and New Mexico Prays on initiatives to help move Albuquerque forward," says Mayor Keller. "The success we have seen through our partnership on Convoy of Hope and Love ABQ has made a huge impact on our city."

Former New Mexico Lt. Governor John Sanchez explains the impact he has seen. "I like to call them parallels of truth. What works in the spiritual world works in the political world. And I think that America Prays will be that means to bridge that gap. So, I would encourage my fellow leaders to reach out and take advantage of this tremendous resource both for them individually and for their teams."

Prayer should make us more like Jesus—and Jesus was the ultimate servant. Jesus declared in Matthew 20:28, "The Son of Man did not come to be served, but to serve and give His life as a ransom for many."

The model of America Prays is to unite the body of Christ in 24/7 prayer. After we lay the foundation of united prayer, we serve our community together.

We have seven prayer focuses that each of our cities, states, and nations adopt, but we also encourage them to choose one or two social issues and serve together to see a transformation in those areas.

In New Mexico, we have focused on poverty and crime. In Oklahoma, we're partnering with Governor Kevin Stitt to improve education.

Our seven prayer focuses are:

1. Pray for unbelievers to be saved.
2. Pray for a national spiritual awakening.
3. Pray for the unity of the church.
4. Pray for families.
5. Pray for racial reconciliation.
6. Pray for life to be valued and protected through all stages of life, beginning at conception.
7. Pray for local and national government leaders.

We also believe churches should unite and proclaim the Gospel. In June 2018, twenty-one churches partnered with Calvary Church and Skip Heitzig for Freedom Celebration, a two-night Gospel crusade where 1,968 people made decisions for Christ.

We desire to be an answer to Jesus' prayer in John 17:21: "That all of them may be one, Father, just as you are in me and I am in you. May they also be in us so that the world may believe that you have sent me." Jesus believed we could experience the same quality of unity He has with the Father. And as my friend Jonathan Friz says, "Jesus is going to get what He prayed for and what He paid for."

Prayer is the language that moves heaven and unites God's people on Earth. A unified church is the most credible witness to the world that Jesus is Lord. We had been asking God to unite the church of New Mexico, and Jesus was beginning to answer that prayer.

We knew that to obtain the favor and blessing of God in our life and ministry, we had to stop building our own kingdom and instead focus on unity with other believers and churches. As Psalm 133 reveals, unity attracts God's blessing and favor. What unites us is greater than what divides us, and we are stronger together.

As our nation is more polarized and divided than at any time since the 1960s, and our partisan politics are tearing us apart, the best way to confront that divisiveness is united prayer.

We have one Father, one Lord, one Spirit, one baptism, and one church, and it's going to take the whole church, united in prayer, to present the Gospel to a broken and hurting world.

CHAPTER 8

A DAILY PURSUIT

§

"Hey, buddy!" Dad exclaimed.

My second semester of college had just started when I received a phone call in the fall of 1992.

"Hey, Dad!" I responded.

Then, in a less enthused voice, he asked, "Do you have a second to talk?"

"Sure. What's up?"

Dad took a deep breath.

"It's about your brother, John. He was arrested last night. The district attorney is going to prosecute him for trafficking cocaine and acid."

What? My big brother—my hero—is a drug dealer? How did that happen?

He graduated from high school at the top of his class and received the Presidential Scholarship to the University of New Mexico. When I left for Bible college, I knew he wasn't living for God, but a drug dealer? I was in complete shock.

The phone felt cold in my hand. I tried to think of what to say, but words failed me.

"Brian, are you there?"

"Yeah, I'm here. I don't know what to say."

"I know. I didn't know what to think at first, either. But listen to me. John needs our prayers. I know you two aren't on great terms, but that doesn't matter. We need to pray for him."

When the call was over, I stood frozen for several minutes. *John is facing five to ten years in prison.*

"Pray for him," my father had implored.

At that moment, I realized I didn't want to. I was afraid. This hit too close to home. Unlike nameless billions across the world, if I prayed for my brother and God didn't answer my prayer, I would know.

The words of my father refused to relent, but I fought back.

"Wouldn't my time be better spent praying for the millions of people who have never even heard your name, Jesus? What about them? My brother has already scorned you. Do you really want me to pray for him?"

In response, the Holy Spirit reminded me of Luke 15:4: "Suppose one of you has a hundred sheep and loses one of them. Doesn't he leave the ninety-nine in the open country and go after the lost sheep until he finds it?"

By a deliberate choice of will, I sank to my knees. The mere thought of praying for my brother burned like blisters on my heart, but I chose to pray for him anyway.

"God, please, help my brother. John is lost, he's running from you, and he needs you. Please draw his heart close to yours and let him know your love," I prayed.

PRAY WITH PASSION

In the days following my call with my dad, I learned to pray with passion. Praying for billions of souls had always been easy. Now, when praying for my brother, I had to embrace pain, fear, and shame.

What if God didn't answer my prayer? What if my brother didn't repent?

I think we're afraid to pray for those we love the most because deep down, we worry we will be disappointed if God doesn't answer our prayers. And so, we don't pray because we don't want to be let down. But I've discovered the more intimate and vulnerable we're willing to get in prayer, the more God can do in our hearts.

As the weeks turned into months and the months to years, my brother's spiritual and physical condition worsened. Thanks to an expensive attorney, John beat the charges for selling cocaine, but that made him even more arrogant and resistant to God's will.

John got involved with the Mexican cartel trafficking drugs into New Mexico. He became addicted to heroin and overdosed over fifteen times. How could I continue to pray passionately for my wayward brother when I could not see progress?

The same year I started praying for John, I picked up a book in my college library entitled *Praying Hyde: Apostle of Prayer*. It was the biography of another John—a missionary to India named John Hyde.

When John Hyde arrived in India in 1892, he discovered there was only one other missionary in the state of Punjab, which had a population of approximately one million people at the time. Winning India for Christ seemed like a daunting task.

In 1908, after sixteen years of missionary work with little fruit to show for his labors, John Hyde changed his strategy. The Holy Spirit challenged John to pray for a whole year for

God to save one soul every day in India. Even though his fellow missionaries thought this was absurd, over 365 people accepted Christ over the next twelve months.

The following year, the Holy Spirit challenged Hyde to stretch his faith and pray for two souls every day. He would often pray all night until he felt confident two people had surrendered their lives to Christ that day.

John shocked his fellow missionaries when he announced in 1910 that he would double his goal yet again and pray for four souls every day. He increased his prayer target once more the following year—*eight souls a day.* Hyde's faith and prayers sparked a revival in the state of Punjab that spread to the rest of India.

What was the secret to his power in prayer? People who knew John watched him pray passionately for the salvation of the lost. He repeated this simple yet powerful phrase with tears streaming down his face: "Give me souls, oh God, or I die!"

I read that and thought to myself, *Oh, yeah, baby!*

I could feel the Holy Spirit asking my heart, "Will you pray for souls with the same passion and urgency of John Hyde?"

Supercharged by John Hyde's ferocity, I accepted the challenge. "Yes, Lord!"

"Will you pray for your brother John like that? Will you weep over him and intercede for his soul every day until he repents and surrenders his life to me?"

I wasn't prepared for that, but I was determined.

"Lord, if you'll pray through me, yes, I'll pray for my brother the way John Hyde prayed for the lost souls of India."

I could pray for John for a few days, and maybe even a few weeks, but how could I sustain that level of intensity in prayer? Where would I find the passion?

That's when the Holy Spirit took me to James 5:16-18: "The earnest prayer of a righteous person has great power and wonderful results. Elijah was as human as we are, and yet when he prayed earnestly that no rain would fall, none fell for the next three and a half years! Then he prayed for rain, and down it poured."[49]

Elijah controlled the weather in Israel because he understood the power of passionate prayer. If you don't care about what you're praying for, why should God care? God responds to passion.

The word *earnest* in Greek means "passionate, active, prevailing, and energetic." Passive prayers have no power whatsoever. Passionate prayers please the heart of a passionate God. The Holy Spirit began teaching me how to pray with passion and urgency, with fire in my bones.

When was the last time you prayed for your family and friends like John Hyde prayed for the lost in India?

Passion is awesome, but I knew I needed more than passion if I was going to spend time with Jesus every day for the rest of my life. I realized I needed discipline and structure.

I read a book in the spring of 1993 that transformed my prayer life. Dick Eastman's book, *The Hour that Changes the World,* divides prayer into 12 five-minute segments:

1. Praise and worship
2. Waiting on the Lord
3. Confession of guilt and sin

4. Praying Scripture
5. Watching
6. Intercession
7. Petitions
8. Thanksgiving
9. Song
10. Contemplation/Meditation
11. Listening
12. Praise

Dick's book gave my prayer life the structure and discipline I had been lacking.

Over the past twenty-eight years, God has continued to teach me more lessons about having a daily quiet time with God, and I want to share a few of those lessons with you.

PURSUE GOD DAILY

The secret to sustaining your love for Christ for a lifetime is to pursue Him daily. Discipline yourself to spend time with God every day. I love how Catholic theologian Henri Nouwen expressed it: "A spiritual life without discipline is impossible. Discipline is the other side of discipleship. The practice of a spiritual discipline makes us more sensitive to the small, gentle voice of God."[50]

The secret to sustaining your love for Christ for a lifetime is to pursue Him daily.

Many people get saved and fall in love with Jesus, but they eventually fall out of love because they fail to develop the spiritual habits and disciplines necessary to grow and sustain their love for Christ. Jesus even warned us that "the love of many will grow cold."[51]

PRAY AN HOUR A DAY

I want to ask you the same question Jesus asked His disciples in Matthew 26:40: "Could you not watch and pray with me for one hour?"[52]

Make it a daily goal to spend at least an hour with God in prayer, worship, Bible study, and meditation—not out of religious duty, but out of delight. You can set aside a whole hour or divide it into thirty minutes in the morning and thirty in the evening or fifteen minutes at a time. Find a rhythm that works for you. Why don't you stop right now and schedule a daily recurring date with God on your mobile phone, tablet, day planner, calendar, or laptop? If you don't plan it, it won't happen.

CHOOSE A DEDICATED TIME

I'm not much of a morning person—never have been—but for the past twenty-eight years, my quiet time with God has been in the morning right after I wake up.

Solomon wrote in Ecclesiastes 3:1, "There is a time for everything, and a season for every activity under heaven." There is a right time for everything—a time to work, a time to play, and a time to pray. Find the right time for your daily devotions with God and fight to keep it.

President George Washington prayed and read the Bible every morning. A French citizen who knew Washington remarked, "Every day of the year, he rises at five in the morning; as soon as he is up, he dresses, then prays reverently to God."[53]

Prayer softens your heart and awakens your conscience. If you don't pray in the morning, it will likely show in the way you treat people. If you don't have time before you leave the house, pray on the way to work or school. Why not maximize your commute time by spending it with God?

Choose a Dedicated Place

Choose a strategic place to pray that offers minimal distractions. Maybe your bedroom, office, living room, backyard, car, a park, the mountains, or my personal favorite— your generous neighbor's hot tub while he's at work.

Jesus taught us to withdraw when we pray: "But when you pray, go into your room, close the door and pray to your Father, who is unseen. Then your Father, who sees what is done in secret, will reward you." (Matthew 6:6)

The prophet Daniel had a dedicated time and place to meet with God. He had an upstairs room where he would pray three times a day with the windows opened toward Jerusalem (Daniel 6:10). Do you have a dedicated place to connect with God?

Prepare Your Heart to Meet with God

Once I am in my prayer spot, the first thing I do is prepare my heart to seek God. I quiet my heart and clear my mind of all distractions, silence my phone, and give God my undivided attention.

As a CEO prepares for a business meeting or a chef prepares the ingredients to cook, it takes effort to get your heart ready to seek God (Ezra 7:10). Turn off the television, your phone, and anything else that might distract you. Follow the wise instruction of Psalm 46:10, "Be still, and know that I am God."

START WITH THANKSGIVING

I start my prayer time by thanking God for all He has done for me. I thank Him for my wife and children, my friends, my ministry, and for His favor, provision, and protection. Thanksgiving is the quickest way to enter God's presence. Psalm 95:2 urges us to "come into His presence with thanksgiving."

Thanking God is the best way to put your problems in perspective. When you begin thanking God for all He has done, your focus shifts from what you *don't have* to what you *do have*, and that changes everything. The more you thank God, the easier it will become.

WORSHIP

After thanking God, I spend some time in worship. Now, by worship, I mean more than singing along to a few songs on my worship playlist. Music can help facilitate worship, but worship is not the music we play or the songs we sing. Worship is the love, adoration, and honor we pour out to God. It's a passionate love relationship with God. Spend some time in personal worship, pouring out your heart and love to God.

And feel free to sing, clap, lift your hands, or dance—whatever helps you connect with God. The primary activity in heaven revealed in Scripture is worship. Why not get a head start on your eternal purpose?

PRAY AND LISTEN TO GOD'S VOICE

Worship naturally flows right into prayer. Talk to God and pour out your heart to Him as you would talk to your best friend.

You don't have to speak to God in King James language—just be open, honest, real, and vulnerable.

When you are happy, let Him know. When you are angry or frustrated, tell Him. God is a big boy—He can handle your honesty. Pray for wisdom to make the right decisions. Ask God to enlarge your capacity to love Him and people in general.

Pray for integrity to guard your heart so you don't dishonor God or your family. Pray for your family, friends, coworkers, neighbors, leaders, and anyone else the Holy Spirit puts on your heart.

After you talk to God, be quiet and listen to Him. It might seem weird and uncomfortable at first to sit there without speaking, but it will get easier the more you do it.

Pastor Robert Morris writes, "If you want to hear God's voice, then you must get to know God as a person—and this takes time and intention, much the same as it takes to know any friend."[54]

There are so many ways God can speak to you. He might put a Bible verse on your heart, lead you to pray for someone, remind you of one of His promises, convict you of sin, comfort you, encourage you, give you a creative idea, or give you peace. But you need to listen.

READ AND LISTEN TO THE BIBLE

I try to spend at least thirty minutes reading the Word and then meditate on it. As I fall asleep at night, I listen to the audio Bible on my phone, starting with John chapter 1. It gives me incredible peace.

Reading the Bible every day is hard work and requires a great deal of effort and discipline. I love how theologian R. C.

Sproul put it: "We fail in our duty to study God's Word not so much because it is difficult to understand, not so much because it is dull and boring, but because it is work. Our problem is not a lack of intelligence or a lack of passion. Our problem is that we are lazy."[55]

Read the Bible slowly. I take my time reading the Scriptures. I would rather read one chapter and understand it than rush through ten chapters and not remember what I read. What matters is not how fast you finish, but how much of the Word you retain and apply. Reflect on the passages you read and their implications for your life. Underline and memorize any verses or phrases that stand out to you.

Read the Bible prayerfully. My friend Mart Green has read the Bible over 8,000 days straight and counting. He prays for four things every day before he reads the Bible. He calls it OIOI prayer:

1. **OPEN:** Psalm 119:18, "Open my eyes that I may see wonderful things in your law."
2. **INSIGHT AND 3. OBEDIENCE:** Psalm 119:34, "Give me insight so that I can do what you tell me—my whole life one long, obedient response.[56]
4. **INTIMACY:** James 4:8, "Draw near to God, and He will draw near to you."[57]

Mart's prayer has become part of my daily routine. Pray for God to open your eyes and give you insight, obedience, and intimacy as you read the Word of God.

Read the Bible as a love letter. When you read the Bible, don't read it as you would a history book, novel, anthology, fantasy, mystery, or self-help book—read it as a love letter from God to you.

The Bible is a true story, but it's also a *love story*. Philosopher G. K. Chesterton expressed it well: "Christianity met the mythological search for romance by being a story, and the philosophical search for truth by being a true story."[58]

Although it shows us how to live the Christian life and walk in God's ways, the Bible is not primarily a how-to manual— it's *a marriage proposal*. One of the central stories of the Bible is a father searching for a bride for his son.

Paul wrote in 2 Corinthians 11:2, "I am jealous for you with a godly jealousy. I promised you to one husband, to Christ, so that I might present you as a pure virgin to Him." The angel said to John in Revelation 21:9, "Come, I will show you the bride, the wife of the Lamb."

When you read the Bible as a love letter from God, it changes how you feel about it, interpret it, and respond to it. You realize that all God's moral laws and commands are not strict regulations from a distant deity meant to spoil your fun but, instead, they are cautions from a loving Father who only wants what is best for you.

God knows that although sin is fun for a season, in the end, it will destroy you and separate you from His presence. And He can't bear the thought of being apart from you. When you approach the Bible from that reality, it changes everything.

Listen to the Bible regularly. The Scriptures were written for an oral society. They were designed to be listened to, and whenever possible, in a community. Few people in Bible times were literate—most of them engaged with the Word of God by listening to it being read out loud and discussed.

The Apostle Paul instructed his disciple Timothy to "devote yourself to the public reading of Scripture, to preaching and to teaching." (1 Tim. 4:13)

Reading even in literate societies like America is on the decline. The percent of Americans who read for pleasure daily has decreased by thirty percent since 2004.[59] It's not that we can't read—it's that we don't read. In this context, helping people engage with the Scriptures by listening to them and watching them becomes even more critical.

Since our kids were young, we have read the Bible to them nearly every day. In the past year, we have begun watching the Lumo videos, which are a visual translation of the four Gospels. These videos have increased our family's engagement with the Bible. You can watch them for free on the Bible.is and YouVersion apps.

About ten years ago, God challenged me to listen to the Bible every night. After our family devotions, I listen to the Gospel of John on my phone. I'm a high energy person, so it takes me a while to fall asleep. I often listen to the whole Gospel of John before I drift off to sleep. The Bible plays all night long, and I wake up to the sound of God's Word.

Listening to the Bible daily has had a considerable impact on my spiritual growth and receptivity to God. I would encourage you not only to read the Scriptures, but to listen to them as well. And as often as you can, listen to the Word of God with others—family, friends, or your small group—and discuss them.

MEDITATE

After reading the Bible, I meditate on it. Some days I'll meditate on a whole chapter or story, other days only a single verse or phrase. Think about what you read, reflect on it, and apply it to your life. Allow the Word of God to convict you, challenge you, correct you, inform you, inspire you, and transform you.

Joshua 1:8 explains the power of Scripture meditation: "Do not let this Book of the Law depart from your mouth; meditate on it day and night, so that you may be careful to do everything written in it. Then you will be prosperous and successful." John Stott wrote, "We must allow the Word of God to confront us, to disturb our security, to undermine our complacency, and to overthrow our patterns of thought and behavior."[60]

The doers of the Word are blessed, not the hearers, admirers, or reciters of the Word. Jesus declared, "Blessed rather are those who hear the Word of God and obey it."[61] The whole point of reading the Bible is to put it into practice. God doesn't want you to *agree* with the Word; He wants you to *obey* the Word.

CONFESS AND REPENT

As I am meditating on the Word, I also reflect on my spiritual condition. I ask God to search my heart and reveal any hidden sin. I pray Psalm 139:23-24 every day: "Search me, O God, and know my heart; test me and know my anxious thoughts. Point out anything in me that offends you and lead me along the path of everlasting life."[62]

Confess all the sins, bad attitudes, and wrong mindsets God reveals to you. 1 John 1:9 explains, "If we confess our sins, He is faithful and just and will forgive us our sins and purify us from all unrighteousness." Remember, though, confession is incomplete without repentance. There's no *forgiveness* of sin without *repentance* of sin.

All lasting change begins with repentance, which means to change the way you think. The real battlefield is in your mind. Every action begins as a thought, and nothing will change in your life until you change the way you think.

If the passage you are reading talks about lustful thoughts, search your heart and see if you've had any in the past week. Repent, and ask God to forgive you and cleanse you. Not out of fear, but because you don't want anything to come between you and God.

JOURNAL

As I am meditating and reflecting, I also journal. Some days I write several pages, other times maybe only a sentence or two. None of my journal entries will ever win a Pulitzer Prize, but that's okay because I don't journal to impress anyone. I journal so I will remember what God has revealed to me through Scripture.

I record promises He gives me and celebrate answered prayers. When I get discouraged, I read my journal, and it reminds me of God's past faithfulness, which provides me with strength and hope for my current challenges. Mercy keeps her diary in one of those fancy leather notebooks. My handwriting is illegible, so I prefer to record my journal on my phone, and I transfer it to my laptop a few times a week.

The prophet stated in Habakkuk 2:2: "Write down the vision; write it clearly on clay tablets so whoever reads it can run to tell others."[63] Keeping a journal is the best way I know to document your journey with God. And you never know, your journal could inspire future generations to serve God.

BE ACCOUNTABLE

I've learned that having a spiritual growth partner to support you and hold you accountable makes all the difference. You can ask your spouse, your pastor, a friend, or a sibling to help you grow spiritually.

Mercy is my primary accountability partner. We pray together every day and hold each other accountable for our relationship with Christ. My friend Bruno Interlandi is my secondary accountability partner. We encourage each other to be the best fathers, husbands, and leaders we can be.

King Solomon illustrated the importance of partnership and accountability in Ecclesiastes 4:9-10: "Two are better than one...If one falls down, his friend can help him up. But pity the man who falls and has no one to help him up!"

Who is holding you accountable for your spiritual growth and Christlike character?

MIX IT UP

I don't know about you, but I'm a creature of habit. I could eat dinner at the same restaurant and watch a movie at the same theater every week. Mercy is the complete opposite. She gets bored with routine and likes to try new things. It must be the artist in her. She helps me keep our dates fresh and unpredictable. The same principle applies to our relationship with God.

Daily habits are essential but be sure to add some variety to your quiet time. Some days you might want to spend more time in prayer and less time reading.

Other days you'll feel drawn to study the Word and won't have much time left for prayer. Sometimes you will worship God the whole time. Feel free to mix it up. You don't have to stick to a specific routine. Don't be afraid to *freestyle*.

FAMILY DEVOTIONS

Mercy and I began having family devotions with our children when Chloe was two, and Colin was a newborn. Now Chloe is sixteen, Colin is fourteen, and Lauren is ten. We read the Bible, discuss it, pray over each other, and worship together.

After our kids pray, I have them repeat a prayer after me that goes something like this: "I love you, Father God. I love you, Jesus. I love you, Holy Spirit. I will love you, serve you, fear you, honor you, and obey you all the days of my life. Give me good dreams, no bad dreams. Cover me with your blood, your peace, and your presence. I will fear no evil for you are with me."

You probably have a television, game console, or an entertainment center somewhere in your home where you gather with your family to relax. But do you have a family altar—a place in your home dedicated to seeking God?

If you're a parent, having devotions with your children is the best thing you can do to raise them in God's ways. Even if your kids are young, they will benefit from family devotions. Even fifteen or twenty minutes in God's presence will make a huge difference in their lives.

Most parents spend insane amounts of money, time, and energy to get their kids to soccer practice, piano lessons, birthday parties, and school events. Those are all great activities, but they have little power to equip your children to fulfill their destiny in Christ.

Proverbs 22:6 instructs parents to "train up a child in the way he should go; even when he is old he will not depart from it."[64] The best investment you can make in your children's future is to help them fall in love with Jesus and the Word of God. Turn off the TV, turn on some worship music, begin praying, and watch heaven invade your home.

GOD STILL ANSWERS PRAYER

It took many years, but God heard my desperate prayers for my brother. John rededicated his life to Christ when he had an encounter with God in solitary confinement at the Santa Fe State Prison in 2008.

Today, John leads a multi-site church, Freedom City Church, in Springfield, Missouri. He's married to Hannah, and they have two children, Brooklyn and Phoenix. He runs five addiction recovery homes and has gone from being a dope dealer to a hope dealer.

God still answers prayer. Don't stop praying. Ephesians 3:20 can become your reality: "God can do anything, you know—far more than you could ever imagine or guess or request in your wildest dreams!"[65]

Tips for Daily Devotions

1. Choose a dedicated time

2. Find a place with few distractions

3. Prepare your heart to meet with God

4. Thank God

5. Worship

6. Pray and listen to God's voice

7. Read the Bible

8. Meditate

9. Repent and confess any known sins

10. Keep a daily journal

11. Find an accountability partner

12. Mix it up and add some variety

CHAPTER 9

YOU DROWNED ME

I gazed out of the airplane window, lost in thought.

It was October 2019, and I was on a flight bound for Rio de Janeiro, Brazil. That summer, America Prays had grown to over 1,200 churches in fourteen states across the United States and had spread to nine nations through our global branch, World Prays. Tens of thousands of people were joining us in prayer.

From my vantage point in the plane, I watched the skyline in the distance and wished my eyes were good enough to see the churches who were partnering with us in Sri Lanka, India, Japan, Mexico, Singapore, Malaysia, Bangladesh, and Argentina.

Brazil would be our 10th country, and I was pumped.

The morning after arriving in Rio, I joined my friends Mark Anderson, Paul Eshelman, Dave Gibson, and David Hamilton at the event center where we would spend the next four days training over 600 Brazilian church leaders in prayer, evangelism, Bible translation, and church planting. My part to play was teaching the prayer track and casting the vision of 24/7 prayer in Brazil. The experience felt surreal.

Back in 2002, when I worked for another ministry, Mercy and I had the opportunity to start branches of our ministry in Brazil, Germany, and Italy.

As we were preparing to speak at a pastors' conference in Napoli in June 2002, the Lord kept us awake all night and asked us to give up the nations for a season and focus entirely on one city—Albuquerque.

We left that ministry, and, for the next seventeen years, our primary focus became serving Albuquerque, uniting churches in our city, and planting our church. Jesus told us that if we sacrifice the nations, one day, He would open the doors to travel again and minister all around the world.

Now, seventeen years later, God was bringing my heart for Brazil and the nations full circle.

After I cast the vision for Brazil Prays, multiple key leaders invited me back to Brazil in 2020 to crisscross the nation and cover every community in 24/7 prayer. And just like that, our 10th World Prays country was launched.

It's crazy how things change. Three-and-a-half years ago, I was screaming at God on the hospital floor next to my daughter. My throat cracked as I cried out day after day for her healing.

I remembered the day God told me it was time to start unceasing prayer. I was afraid and struggled to believe such a movement was possible. I chose to follow but was terrified and felt unqualified and incompetent. I prayed, but often with only silence in response.

And yet, through it all, God never failed to prove himself trustworthy. Chloe walked out of the hospital two days after the neurologist told us she would never walk again. And though her full recovery would still take several years, God remained faithful every step of the journey. When I had no idea how we would even start a prayer movement in Albuquerque, God was opening doors to the nations.

The year 2019 was packed with doors swinging wide open. Gregg Hull, the Mayor of Rio Rancho, New Mexico, asked me to lead his faith advisory council and partner for city transformation.

I was able to spend some time in Orlando and develop a friendship with Steve Douglass the President of Cru. Steve was very kind and gracious to endorse America Prays.

"Campus Crusade for Christ was launched in 1951 with a special emphasis on prayer. And through the years, we have persisted in believing that God is the essential key to any success we might experience. So continually calling on Him in prayer is our most important activity. That's why I am so excited to support America Prays and their vision of uniting and equipping 40,000 churches in 24/7 prayer for a national spiritual awakening.

"I am especially grateful for my friend Brian Alarid and the other leaders of this movement that began in America and is now spreading to many nations through World Prays. I encourage you to go to AmericaPrays.org and explore how you and your church or ministry might benefit from what America Prays has to offer."

In May, we saw over 1,500 believers unite in prayer for the National Day of Prayer. We served the city for a whole week in June through Love ABQ, blessing the city with over 3,000 volunteer hours.

Governor Stitt called me at the end of June and asked if we could partner to cover Oklahoma in 24/7 prayer. At a conference in Tulsa, I connected with Pete Greig, the founder of 24-7 Prayer International and author of *Red Moon Rising*, and four of his senior leaders. We began a friendship and partnership that continues to grow.

We partnered with Mark Anderson at the Museum of the Bible in Washington D.C. to launch All America, which is a ten-year initiative to mobilize the body of Christ to pray for every American by name, share the Gospel with them, engage them with the Bible, and invite them into a Christian community.

We hosted a conference for Native American women with Navajo President Jonathan Nez and First Lady Phefelia Nez and Vice President Myron Lizer and Second Lady Dottie Lizer.

And the year wasn't even over yet.

We partnered with the City of Albuquerque, Comcast, Chick-fil-A, Presbyterian Healthcare, ESPN radio, and over 100 businesses, churches, nonprofits, and government agencies for our second Convoy of Hope outreach at the Albuquerque Convention Center on November 2, 2019. We had 9,248 people in attendance, including volunteers.

We gave away over 12,000 meals, 9,800 bags of groceries, 1,962 pairs of children's shoes, 5,000 pairs of socks, 1,600 gardens in a bag, 840 family portraits, and 425 haircuts. Over 2,200 people received health care services, and the National Breast Cancer Foundation served 1,600 women. And the most amazing part was that 4,506 people requested prayer, and 105 people indicated they wanted to accept Jesus as their Savior.

We launched Oklahoma Prays with our friends Brian and Marla Hill, Pastor Clarence Hill, and Mart Green on the top floor of the Devon Tower in Oklahoma City. Over 250 pastors and leaders joined us. It even made the local news.

We are partnering with Mayor Keller and the City of Albuquerque to offer parenting classes, marriage classes, addiction recovery classes, and financial stewardship classes in community centers across our city. "With New Mexico Prays bringing additional programing to our community centers, we will be able to fill a huge need in the community providing access to training and resources," Mayor Keller testifies. "This partnership is allowing us to expand our offering of services to families who need it most."

Pastor Randy Frazee and I spent time dreaming about mobilizing hundreds of churches to cover Kansas City in 24/7 prayer. And if I know anything, it's that God is just getting started.

The more I continue to trust God, the more I see Him come through, and the more I see Him come through, the more I dare to trust Him. Hudson Taylor, the missionary to China, explained it best: "When I cannot read, when I cannot think, when I cannot even pray, I can trust."

God is teaching me to trust Him, and this whole experience reminds me of when I taught my youngest daughter, Lauren, to swim.

When Lauren was four years old, we got in the pool, and I laid her on her back, my arm underneath her.

"Head back, belly up, deep breath," I instructed. "I'm going to let go of you, and you are going to float all by yourself, okay, sweetheart?"

"Okay, Daddy."

I let go, and half a millisecond later, she began flailing her arms and screaming. Down she went.

I was only inches away, and immediately I grabbed her and carried her out of the pool. She was coughing up water, and Mercy picked her up and began patting her on the back.

"Daddy, you drowned me. You drowned me!" Lauren yelled through gasping breaths.

"Lauren, I was right next to you the whole time. I wasn't going to let anything bad happen to you, I promise," I tried to reassure her.

"Mommy, Mommy, Daddy drowned me!"

I put my arms out to hold her, and for the first time in her life, Lauren refused me.

"No, you tried to kill me!" she screamed. That drew some uncomfortable looks from the lifeguard and families at the community center pool. It took six months before Lauren would trust me to take her in the pool again, but now, six years later, she's the best swimmer in the family.

Hebrews 4:11 instructs us to *strive* to trust God and enter into His rest. That seems counterintuitive. Exhaust every effort to enter into rest.

Spiritual rest is similar to swimming: The same water that has the potential to drown you can also cause you to float, if you will relax and put your head back, take a deep breath and trust the oxygen in your lungs. The human lungs function as natural buoys—when filled with air, they rise to the surface of the water.

God promises us in Isaiah 43:2, "When you cross deep rivers, I will be with you, and you won't drown. When you walk through the fire, you won't be burned or scorched by the flames."[66] If you trust God's hand, the very thing the enemy sends to drown you will cause you to float.

Remember, no weapon formed against you will prosper (Isaiah 54:17). That doesn't mean weapons won't be formed or launched against you, but they won't wipe you out. God is your defense and your protector.

In July 2019, our largest donor notified us they wouldn't be able to support us that year. I would have freaked out and panicked in years past, but this time the Lord reminded me, "Have I ever let you drown before?" He hadn't, so again, I chose to trust Him. I knew I was following God's will, and so I decided to rest and pray in faith. Four days later, an anonymous donation came in that was equal to the amount our largest donor had given us the year before.

God doesn't always do things that way. Sometimes, an anonymous donation *doesn't* come through because God's plan is bigger than that—like our family's battle for Chloe's life and health. In some ways, that's an even bigger miracle, but it's often more confusing at first.

I bet you've had your own epic battles with fear, doubt, anger, frustration, and disillusionment with God. You're trying to serve God to the best of your ability, striving to do the right thing, but God feels like he is a million miles away.

God, can't you see what's happening to me? Where are you, Lord? Don't you care about me? With one snap of your fingers, you could fix all this brokenness, heal all this sickness, right every wrong—and yet for some reason, you choose not to intervene, and I don't get it. Why God?

Have you ever sought God with your whole heart, for weeks, months, or even years, and dared to believe in the power of prayer, only to be disappointed? Disappointment with God is a universal experience that no one is immune from, not even those who are closest to God.

Mary and Martha sent word for Jesus to come to pray for their brother Lazarus.

"Lord, the one you love is sick," John 11:3 reads.

Surely, Jesus will come in time to heal Lazarus. After all— Mary and Martha conclude—Jesus loves him like His own brother. Jesus indicated He would come, but then He delayed His trip, and by the time He arrived, Lazarus had been dead and buried for four days.

As Jesus approached, Martha rushed out to meet Him. "Lord, if you had been here, my brother would not have died!"

Do you hear what Martha is saying? In essence, she's saying, "You're a little late, Jesus, don't you think?"

She wasn't the first or the last person to think that.

Sometimes when people pray, things still can go from bad to worse. Sometimes, you pray and trust God, only to feel as if you've been let down.

You pray, but your marriage still ends in divorce.

You pray, but your company still goes bankrupt.

You pray, but your ministry still closes.

You pray, but your dreams still crash and burn.

You pray, but your twelve-year-old daughter still spends every day crying in pain.

You pray in faith, but sometimes Lazarus still dies.

Is prayer just some meaningless charade? If prayer isn't going to change the outcome, why pray? I mean, is it even worth it?

Well, is it possible we've missed the whole point of prayer? What if prayer is less about changing outcomes and more about transforming our hearts? What if prayer is less about victory and more about learning to surrender to God?

What if prayer is more about alignment than alleviation? Prayer is more about aligning our hearts and minds with God's will than alleviating pain and suffering.

What if prayer is more about learning to trust Jesus than it is about Jesus doing something for us? We must remember that Jesus isn't our genie in a bottle. God doesn't exist to answer our prayers—we exist for Him. The primary outcome of prayer is that God transforms us into the image of Christ as we learn to trust Him.

PRAYER IS TRANSFORMATION.

Prayer is less about changing people and circumstances and more about transforming you into the image of Christ.

As you behold God's glory in prayer, He transforms you into His image. Paul explained in 2 Corinthians 3:18, "And we all, who with unveiled faces contemplate the Lord's glory, are being transformed into His image with ever-increasing glory, which comes from the Lord, who is the Spirit."

No matter what situation you find yourself in, I hope you can learn the same lesson God has continued to teach me at every turn of the journey: "The one who calls you is faithful, and He will do it." (1 Thess. 5:24)

But please remember, you can't disconnect trust from faith. Trust is resting in Jesus' promise to come through; faith is acting in expectation of that promise.

Jesus proclaims in John 15:7, "But if you remain in me and my words remain in you, you may ask for anything you want, and it will be granted!"

At first glance, it appears as if Jesus is giving us a blank check and telling us we can fill it in any way we want. But you can't separate faith from God's will.

1 John 5:14 clarifies: "This is the confidence we have in approaching God: that if we ask anything according to His will, He hears us."

Jesus did not give us a blank check—He gave us a mission and artillery support to fulfill it.

The condition to answered prayer is that we must pray *according to His will.* When you pray according to God's purpose, you will receive whatever you ask for—maybe not instantly, but you will receive it in God's perfect time.

PRAYER IS TRUST.

It's not about your ability to make it happen, but your willingness to trust God to make it happen.

Prayer is not about your ability to make things happen, but your willingness to place your trust and faith in God.

"Though He slay me, yet will I trust Him."
—Job 13:15 (NKJV)

CHAPTER 10

BREAK ME OFF A PIECE OF THAT KIT KAT BAR

"Hello, my name is Mercy," said the gentle yet confident voice on the other end of the telephone.

It was a snowy Saturday afternoon in January 1995. I was now an associate pastor at the Bible college I had attended.

"I'm a foreign student from Honduras. I'm at LaGuardia Airport in New York City, and I need directions to your Bible college."

"Hi, Mercy. My name is Brian Alarid. So, your name is Misericordia, right?" (Mercy in Spanish is *misericordia*.)

"No, my name is Mercy," she responded adamantly.

There was something special about her voice, even magical. My mind was racing a million miles a minute, trying to figure out what it was.

"What's your middle name?" To this day, I still have no clue why I asked her that. It's been said that the universe contains protons, neutrons, electrons, and *morons*. I was the latter.

"Nicole."

"You mean to tell me that your parents gave you two English names? Are you serious? Your name is Mercy Nicole?"

I thought to myself, *What's wrong with you, man? Stop badgering this poor girl about her name and give her the directions.*

But I couldn't help myself. I had to know more.

"Yes, that's right," answered Mercy in a frustrated tone. "Now, can I please get directions to your college? It's snowing, and I'm standing outside without a winter jacket, putting quarters into a payphone."

And then it happened.

"She's the one," whispered the Holy Spirit inside my heart. "She's your wife."

I beg your pardon. Is that you, Lord? Am I imagining this, or are you speaking to me?

This is what God had been trying to tell me for several weeks. Let me rewind the story about a month.

I was preaching in Acapulco, Mexico, and the nightly services were going well until I contracted a nasty intestinal infection, commonly known as *Montezuma's revenge.*

I spent three dreadful days in bed with diarrhea, abdominal cramps, and a puke bucket next to me. You know you're in bad shape when you start throwing up Gatorade.

The pastor who was hosting me took me to see his doctor, who diagnosed me with severe dehydration. He told me that I would have died in the next twenty-four hours without proper medical care.

As I was lying in bed the next day, trying to keep down as many liquids as I could, the Lord whispered to me, "You will know her by her voice."

"What's *that* supposed to mean, Lord?"

God repeated the message. "You will know your wife by her voice."

"I still don't understand what you're trying to tell me, God. How will I know my wife by her voice? Is she a singer?"

Come on, Lord, throw me a bone here. I'm begging you.

But apparently, Jesus didn't think I needed any more clarity at that point. Over the next few weeks, I tried to discern what God meant by, "You will know her by her voice."

Then it all clicked in one split-second. The voice on the other end of the phone belonged to my future wife. She was the woman who God had tailor-made for me. Mercy was my helpmate, my better half, the missing part of me. She was everything I never knew I always wanted.

But was she hot? That was the only question my carnal mind could focus on. She was God's first choice for me, but what if I wasn't attracted to her?

After I finished giving her directions to our college, I said to the Lord, "I sure hope she's good-looking. That's all I have to say!"

Later that evening, Mercy walked into my college campus as I was heading into the gym to play volleyball.

Mama Mía, sopapilla! Break me off a piece of that Kit Kat bar. She was the incarnation of all loveliness. Of all the Bible schools in all the towns in all the world, she walked into mine.

"Hello, Brian. It's great to meet you and put a face to your voice finally. I'm Mercy."

She had me at hello.

For some strange reason, neither a full-body embrace nor a passionate kiss seemed appropriate at that moment. So, I extended my hand, instead, and greeted Mercy cordially. There was no doubt in my mind this sun-kissed goddess would be my wife one day.

Now, I wasn't the only one who received a surprise message from the Lord that day. While we were on the phone, Mercy had a strong impression from the Holy Spirit that I was going to be her future husband.

When Mercy first locked eyes with me in the Bible college hallway that evening, Hebrews 5:13 came to her mind, "For he is a *babe*..." One look at me, and she knew I was the one for her.

Over the next two years, I chased Mercy until she caught me. On February 3, 1996, I got down on one knee and professed my undying love for her. I was just a boy, standing in front of a girl, asking her to love me.

We tied the knot in April 1997 and have been happily married ever since. We experienced love at *first sound* before we experienced love at *first sight*. God longs to talk to you and guide you through the most important decisions of your life.

Just watch out for Montezuma.

That experience marked me for life. Since hearing God's voice about who He wanted me to marry, I've sought to make listening to God's voice a daily practice.

In my twenty-six years as a pastor, one question has surfaced the most: "How do you hear the voice of God?" There's a longing in the heart of God's children to talk to their Heavenly Father and hear His voice. Jesus declared in John 10:27, "My sheep listen to my voice; I know them, and they follow me." The Greek word Jesus used for voice is *phóné*—it means a voice or sound. Jesus made it clear His followers should hear and recognize not only His Word but also His voice.

The Bible is the primary way God speaks to His children, but it's not the only way. But before we go farther, let me make it clear that the voice of God will never contradict the Word of God.

Authors Henry Blackaby and Claude King explain it best: "If anything is clear from a reading of the Bible, this fact is clear: God speaks to His people. He spoke to Adam and Eve in the Garden of Eden in Genesis. He spoke to Abraham and the other patriarchs.[67]

God spoke to the judges, kings, and prophets. God was in Christ Jesus speaking to the disciples. God spoke to the early church, and God spoke to John on the Isle of Patmos in Revelation. God does speak to His people, and you can anticipate that He will be speaking to you also."

The phrases "the Lord said" and "God said" occur hundreds of times in the Bible. God spoke to His people in Bible times, and He's still speaking to His people today.

If God has the audacity to call Himself our Father, what kind of father would He be if He never communicated with His children? The Bible shows us hundreds of examples of ordinary people who heard God's voice, and it forever changed their lives. God never changes—He remains the same forever (Malachi 3:6). And He longs to talk to you today just as He did the people in the Bible.

Prayer is a conversation with God. Brother Lawrence remarked, "There is not in the world a kind of life more sweet and delightful than that of a continual conversation with God."[68]

Now, in a conversation, both people take turns talking and listening. Prayer is meant to be a dialogue, not a monologue—an intimate conversation between two people.

Prayer is meant to be a dialogue, not a monologue— an intimate conversation between two people.

If you're doing all the talking, you're missing out on the best part of prayer: hearing God speak to you. Don't be a conversation hog with God. What God has to say to you is more important than what you have to say to Him.

Araminta Ross was born on a Maryland plantation in 1822. Born into slavery, she endured terrible whippings, hard labor, starvation, and abuse, including a fractured skull when she was a teenager.

Araminta escaped to freedom in 1849, making the treacherous journey to Philadelphia all by herself. Instead of enjoying her newfound freedom, she risked her life to free other slaves.

She changed her name to Harriet Tubman and became the most famous conductor in the Underground Railroad Network, which was dedicated to freeing slaves.

Harriet earned the moniker "Moses" for rescuing over 70 slaves. After she led slaves across the border into freedom, she would say, "Glory to God and Jesus, too. One more soul is safe."[69] During the Civil War, she was the first woman to lead an armed expedition, liberating 750 slaves at the Raid on Combahee Ferry in 1863.

What gave Harriet, standing barely five feet tall, her incredible courage and strength?

Harried testified, "I prayed to God to make me strong and able to fight, and that's what I've always prayed for ever since."[70]

Fellow abolitionist Thomas Garrett testified of Harriet, "I never met with any person, of any color, who had more confidence in the voice of God, as spoken direct to her soul. She has frequently told me that she talked with God, and He talked with her every day of her life."[71]

According to Harriet, "It wasn't me; it was the Lord. I always told Him, 'I trust you. I don't know where to go or what to do, but I expect you to lead me,' and He always did."[72]

It was her prayer life and dependence on God's guidance that enabled Harriet to make such a profound impact on American history. When she passed away at the age of ninety, her last words were, "I go to prepare a place for you."[73] In the end, Harriet was still on mission.

God longs to talk to you and lead as He did Harriet. Are you listening?

A STILL SMALL VOICE

The voice of God is powerful and majestic. Sometimes He speaks to His people in a strong, towering voice like when He spoke to Moses out of the burning bush. At other times, God speaks to His children in a gentle whisper.

After Elijah's confrontation with Jezebel and subsequent depression in 1 Kings chapter 19, he was desperate to hear God's voice. He hiked to the top of Mount Horeb, expecting God to appear to him in some demonstrative way. And God didn't disappoint. He caused a strong windstorm to come upon the mountain, and it began tearing the mountain apart.

Elijah probably thought, *Now, that's what I'm talking about. God is about to speak to me out of the windstorm.*

But God wasn't in the windstorm.

God brought an earthquake that shook the mountain to its core. That would have scared most people, but not Elijah. He was sure God was going to appear to him out of the earthquake. This was the moment for which he had been waiting, and yet God wasn't in the earthquake either.

God was just getting warmed up. After the earthquake, He sent a massive wildfire that consumed everything in its path. Elijah was familiar with fire—this was his comfort zone. He told the prophets of Baal, "The god who answers by fire—He is God."

Okay, this makes sense. God wasn't in the windstorm or earthquake, but now He is going to appear to me and speak to me out of the fire as He did with Moses. I'm ready, Lord. Lay it on me!

But much to his surprise, God wasn't in the fire either. God spoke to the prophet in the way he least expected—in a gentle whisper. "And after the earthquake a fire; but the LORD was not in the fire: and after the fire a still small voice" (1 Kings 19:12).

The Hebrew word translated *still small voice* means "a whisper or gentle silence." The God of fire and thunder and lightning and earthquakes is also the God of the gentle whisper.

We can easily miss His voice if we don't listen carefully. In this digital world, information overload bombards us. Quiet your spirit and tune out all the external and internal noise so you can hear God's voice.

I believe most Christ-followers long to hear God's voice, but they aren't sure how to recognize it and distinguish it from their own voice. Does Scripture show us how to hear the voice of God?

The prophet Isaiah heard God speak to him in profound ways. He recorded prophecies that were fulfilled hundreds of years later, including the prophecy about Jesus being born of a virgin. In Isaiah 50:4-5, we see four keys to hearing God's voice:

"The Sovereign Lord has given me an instructed tongue, to know the word that sustains the weary. He wakens me morning by morning, wakens my ear to listen like one being taught. The Sovereign Lord has opened my ears; I have not been rebellious; I have not turned away."

1. Pray every morning. Isaiah stated that God awakened his ear every morning. Before you go to work, the gym, or to school, spend some quiet time with God reading His Word and listening to His voice. It will make a massive impact on the rest of your day.

Author E. M. Bounds shared this insight about morning prayer: "The men who have done the most for God in this world have been early on their knees. He who fritters away the early morning, its opportunity and freshness, in other pursuits than seeking God will make poor headway seeking Him the rest of the day. If God is not first in our thoughts and efforts in the morning, He will be in the last place the remainder of the day."[74]

2. Expect God to speak to you. Isaiah woke up every morning, expecting to hear God speak to him. He said God awakened his "ear to listen."

Your expectations frame your experience. Jesus made this exact point in Matthew 9:29: "According to your faith, let it be done to you." You receive according to the level of your expectations. If you pray but don't expect God to speak to you, He probably won't. It becomes a self-fulfilling prophecy.

3. Listen to God's voice and be ready to be taught.
Isaiah declared, "He wakens my ear to listen like one being taught." In addition to expecting God to speak to you, your attitude will determine whether you hear God's voice. When he prayed, Isaiah took the posture of a student who was eager and ready to learn from his favorite teacher.

Show up to your prayer time with your Bible and journal, ready to take notes. God speaks to you to inform you, educate you, and transform you. Why should God speak to you if you aren't ready to learn?

When the student is ready, the teacher will appear. (Who knew fortune cookies could contain so much wisdom?)

There's a vast difference between hearing and listening. The problem is that we hear, but we don't listen. Listening implies we incline our ear to pay attention so we can remember the message (Isaiah 55:3).

Renowned Christian speaker and author John Ortberg explains why we have such a hard time hearing God: "One reason why we fail to hear God speak is that we are not attentive. We suffer from what might be called 'spiritual mindlessness.'"[75]

Now, you can't force God to speak to you, but you can position yourself to hear Him speak. God longs to talk to you. The question is—are you listening?

Do you pray every day, watching and waiting for the sound of His voice? Do you wait patiently for the Holy Spirit to speak to you? Are you willing to linger in God's presence to wait for Him to talk to you? Ecclesiastes 8:3 warns us, "Do not be in a hurry to leave the king's presence."

So much internal noise from work, the media, and our negative self-talk makes it difficult for us to hear God's voice. You need to clear the spiritual junk out of your life, quiet all the ambient noise, and listen to God's voice.

4. When you hear God speak, obey Him. Isaiah proclaimed, "I have not been rebellious; I have not turned away." The New American Standard Bible translates it, "I was not disobedient."

When God speaks to you, He expects you to obey Him. Jesus stated in Luke 11:28, "Blessed rather are those who hear the word of God and obey it." You need to listen to God and apply it to your personal life. Job 5:27 instructs us to "hear it and apply it to yourself."

If you don't obey God when He speaks to you, He will stop talking to you at some point. If you are unable to hear God's voice right now, ask yourself if you have obeyed the last word God gave you. Obey the last message God gave you, and He will start speaking to you again.

Four Keys to Hearing God's Voice:
1. Pray every morning.
2. Expect God to speak to you.
3. Listen to God's voice and be ready to be taught.
4. When you hear God speak, obey Him.

As my good friend, *El Guapo,* would say, "The Lord speaks to us in a *plethora* of ways." There's not a "right way" to hear God's voice. God is so big and diverse that there are myriads of ways He can speak to you. Hebrews 1:1 confirms this, "In the past, God spoke to our ancestors through the prophets at many times and in various ways."

We're all wired differently, and God speaks to us in ways we can understand. I would be willing to bet Bill Gates' last dollar you've heard the voice of God. But perhaps you didn't recognize it because it didn't sound like Charlton Heston or come out of a burning bush.

In his book, *Whisper*, Mark Batterson reveals seven main ways God speaks to us. "God speaks through His word. That's our starting point. He whispers to us through doors, dreams, and desires. He converses with us through promptings, pain, and other people."[76]

In my personal Bible studies, I've found several ways God speaks to people:

- The Bible (Rom. 15:4; 1 Thess. 2:13)
- His voice (1 Kgs. 19:12; Jn. 10:2-5; 10:27)
- Visions, images, and mental pictures (Gen. 46:2; Acts 2:17; 11:5; 18:9; Jer. 1:11-16; 24:3-9)
- Dreams (1 Kings 3:5; Matthew 1:20)
- Angels (Gen. 31:11; Lk. 1:19; Heb. 1:14; 13:2)
- Leaders, mentors, and advisers (2 Chron. 20:20; Acts 11:28; 21:10; Prov. 11:14; 15:22)
- Signs and wonders (Mk.16:20; Acts 2:43; Heb. 2:4)
- Creative ideas (Ex. 31:1-6; Prov. 8:12; Amos 6:5)
- Strategy (Lk. 14:28-30; Prov. 2:11; 21:5)
- Creation and nature (Psa. 8:3-6; Rom. 1:20)
- Natural examples and illustrations (Acts 21:10-11; Mk. 11:12-13; Jer. 13:1-11)
- Internal warnings (Mt. 2:22; Heb. 11:7; 12:25)

- Perceptions (Acts 27:9-11; 1 Sam. 3:8; Lk. 5:22)
- Circumstances (Prov. 3:5-6; Psa. 37:3; Rom. 8:28)
- Peace or lack of peace (Col. 3:15)
- Pain (Job 1-2)

I'm sure you will find many more as you study the Word. You can't limit a limitless God to only speak in a certain way. God speaks to us in our spirit, thoughts, and emotions. He speaks to us through friends and strangers, pastors and leaders, our spouse and children, good people and bad people. He speaks to us through nature and life, prayer and meditation, praise and worship, and, most of all, through His Word. And don't say God doesn't speak to you if your Bible remains unopened, collecting dust on the bookshelf.

Over the years, I've developed a few tests to make sure I hear from God accurately. I believe they will help you as well.

1. God's voice never contradicts God's Word. You must filter everything you hear and feel through the Word of God. If it doesn't align with Scripture, you must reject it. That's how you make sure your *subjective* hearing becomes *objective*. Don't judge what you hear by how many goosebumps you feel; judge it by God's Word.

If what you hear contradicts God's Word, the Holy Spirit isn't speaking to you. God made this clear in Psalm 89:34: "I will not violate my covenant or alter the word that went forth from my lips."

Henry and Richard Blackaby observed: "When God speaks, He does not give new revelation about Himself that contradicts what He has already revealed in Scripture. Rather, God speaks to give application of His Word to the specific circumstances in your life.

When God speaks to you, He is not writing a new book of Scripture, rather, He is applying to your life what He has already said in His Word.

Throughout the Bible, whenever God spoke to someone, that person's life was never the same again. The same is true today. Our prayer is that as you listen to what God is saying to you, you will respond in love and obedience and your life will be transformed as well."[77]

The more you read the Bible, the better you will be able to discern if God is speaking to you.

2. God's voice never tempts you to sin. Christians say some idiotic stuff. For instance, one guy made this comment to me, "I felt like God was telling me to go lay hands on that young girl, and just, you know, show her the love of God."

Give me a break, *Rico Suave!* Did God also tell you to rub her back and invite her out for dinner afterward?

God's voice is pure and holy, and it will never lead you into temptation. If the voice you hear is provoking you to sin, it's either the devil or your sinful nature, not the voice of God. James 1:13 confirms this: "When tempted, no one should say, 'God is tempting me.' For God cannot be tempted by evil, nor does He tempt anyone."

3. God's voice convicts you but never condemns you. The voice of the enemy will remind you of your sin. He will throw your past failures in your face to shame you and condemn you. The Holy Spirit, on the other hand, will convict you of sin but will never make you feel condemned or worthless. Tune out the voice of condemnation and listen to God correct you in love and bring out the best in you.

Paul wrote in Romans 8:1, "Therefore, there is now no condemnation for those who are in Christ Jesus." When God speaks to us, He always gives us hope and courage to face the future.

4. God's voice empowers you to do His will. Whenever people in the Bible heard God's voice, it empowered them to accomplish God's will. His voice guided Noah to build an ark and sustained him for 120 years as he endured all kinds of mocking and reproach.

God's voice enabled Moses to part the Red Sea. God's primary concern is for His will to be accomplished on Earth as it is in heaven, and He's always looking for willing vessels who will partner with Him to perform His will.

5. God's voice is confirmed by God's people. One of the dangers and pitfalls of pursuing God's voice is people can succumb to pride. Be careful not to think you're the only person who hears from God.

If what you hear *is* from God, you have nothing to fear by submitting it to other godly people who also hear God's voice. God created a safety net to keep us on the right path—a multitude of counselors. Solomon explained it this way, "Where there is no guidance the people fall, but in abundance of counselors there is victory."[78]

Paul stated in 2 Corinthians 13:1, "Every matter must be established by the testimony of two or three witnesses."

People who are being led by the Holy Spirit have the humility to submit what they hear to others because they recognize they are not infallible.

No one gets it right 100 percent of the time; that's why we need each other. As the poet John Donne wrote, "No man is an island, entire of itself. Every man is a piece of the continent, a part of the main."

The people of the Bible heard the God of the Bible speak to them personally, and so can you. One word from God can instantly set you free from depression and deliver you from an ugly addiction.

God's voice can fill you with love, courage, hope, faith, and strength. One Spirit-anointed word can transform the hardest of sinners into the most obedient follower of Christ.

Jesus stated in Mark 4:9, "Whoever has ears to hear, let them hear." What God wants to say to you is more valuable than what you have to say to Him. God has many promises and insights He wants to reveal to you. But you must become an active listener to hear His voice.

Pastor Jack Hayford explains: "Then comes the stringer, the point: 'He who has ears to hear, let him hear.' And it's right there that the Master's words issue timeless terms for knowing God's Word—really knowing it: You have to be a genuine listener. That's what 'having ears to hear' means."[79]

One of the first verses I memorized with my children was Matthew 4:4 because I wanted them to experience the thrill of hearing God speak to them from a young age. "It is written: 'Man shall not live on bread alone, but on every word that comes from the mouth of God.'"

As believers, we live on every word that proceeds out of God's mouth. Feed yourself spiritually every day with the Word of God and the voice of God. Jesus loves you and longs to share the secrets of His heart with you. Your part is to listen to His voice. Without His voice and promptings, the Christian life becomes lonely and boring.

God wants to guide you by His voice, as He declared in Isaiah 30:21: "Whether you turn to the right or to the left, your ears will hear a voice behind you, saying, 'This is the way; walk in it.'"

When the Holy Spirit leads you, your life will be better than fiction. When you follow God's promptings, He will take you places you never dreamed possible. Being led by the Holy Spirit is the most thrilling adventure this side of eternity. You are never too old or too young to hear God's voice. All you have to do is listen.

Jesus declared in Revelation 3:20, "Here I am! I stand at the door and knock. If anyone hears my voice and opens the door, I will come in and eat with that person, and they with me."

Right now, Jesus is knocking on the door of your heart. The question is: Will you hear His voice and invite Him to come in and fellowship with you?

CHAPTER 11

A HOUSE OF PRAYER

"You do not judge a church's health by its seating capacity, but by its sending capacity; not by how many people sit in the auditorium, but by how many are sent to the mission field."

Pastor Rick Warren, the author of *The Purpose Driven Life*, projected his voice across the conference table. I had joined my friends Mark Anderson, Steve Douglass, Bob Varney, Paul Eshelman, Dave Gibson, and several others at the Saddleback Ranch in San Juan Capistrano, California.

Warren's words carried truth and those at the table, including me, leaned in closer to hear as he continued: "You judge a church's effectiveness like an army's: not by how many eat in the mess hall, but by how many are out there on the front line."

That was October 2019. Fast-forward two months, and I was back in Orange County, this time at Saddleback Church for the Finishing the Task Conference. For the second year in a row, Saddleback Church granted Dick Eastman and me access to one of their classrooms to spend three days in prayer during the conference, along with our friend Wesley Tullis. We prayed for each other, our families, America, the nations, and revival and spiritual awakening.

As we began our second day of prayer together at Saddleback on December 4, 2019, Eastman looked up and searched my eyes for a long moment.

"Brian, I believe the Lord just gave me an idea."

I listened curiously.

"Our ministry, Every Home for Christ, has 8,000 paid staff, 90,000 volunteers, and 185 offices in 150 nations. If each of our national offices adopted a monthly day of prayer, and all our staff took an hour of prayer, we could cover 150 nations in 24/7 prayer."

I didn't know what to say.

"Will you and World Prays partner with us to help make that happen?" he asked.

Overcome by yet another of God's miraculous breakthroughs, I nodded with tears in my eyes.

"Absolutely. One hundred percent yes. Let's do this together!"

We started with five churches in Albuquerque on January 1, 2017. Three years later, we're partnering with other ministries to launch 24/7 prayer in 150 nations. There is no god like our God!

PRAYER AND MISSION

As we prayed, Rick Warren's words continued to echo in my mind—*You judge a church's health not by its seating capacity, but by its sending capacity.*

I recalled the words of Jesus in John 20:21, "As the Father has sent me, I am sending you." God wants to send you to the broken and hurting in your community and around the world. And yet, so often, we refuse to follow our call. I wondered about it.

The greatest missionary and volunteer forces in the world are sitting on the sidelines in churches watching the world around them go to hell. What can move Christians from being spectators to starting players in the highest-stakes game on Earth: the salvation and discipleship of the world?

The answer occurred to me as it had many times before, something so simple we often overlook it—prayer. Throughout history, God has used prayer to give His people a burden for the unsaved.

The New Testament church was birthed in a prayer meeting, but the power of the Spirit didn't stay in the prayer room. It moved the disciples to the streets of Jerusalem to share the Gospel, and as Acts 2:41 proclaims, 3,000 people responded and were water baptized that day.

And it didn't stop there. Throughout the book of Acts, we see prayer and mission interwoven together, fueling each other. The book of Acts is the story of what happened in between prayer meetings.

The more the disciples prayed, the more they shared their faith. And the more they shared their faith, the more it brought them back to their knees to pray for God's continued courage and boldness to witness for Him.

Real prayer always moves us to mission, and mission drives us to prayer. This is what happened in the Moravian community. After they started 24/7 prayer, the Holy Spirit moved on their hearts to reach the lost, and they sent missionaries all around the world.

Prayer and reaching people far from God are always intricately connected. When you commune with God in prayer, He gives you His heart for the lost.

That is why prayer is not the end game—mission is.

Jesus didn't say, "Go into all the world and make *intercessors* of all nations." He said, "Go into all the world and make *disciples* of all nations."

What do I mean by mission? Mission is sharing the love and Good News of Jesus Christ with people who are far from God. That includes evangelism, compassionate service, cross-cultural missions, and one-on-one discipleship.

The mission is to share Jesus with a broken and hurting world. And your mission field is right where you live, work, and play. God calls some people as missionaries to foreign nations, but He calls everyone to be a bold witness and force for good. God has given you a circle of influence and wants to use you to impact those people for eternity. You can reach people I can never reach.

Dick Eastman often makes this statement, "The degree to which prayer is mobilized is the degree to which the world will be evangelized," and I've found that to be true.

The secret to reaping a harvest of souls is prayer, as Jesus stated in Matthew 9:37-38, "The harvest is plentiful, but the laborers are few; therefore pray earnestly to the Lord of the harvest to send out laborers into his harvest."[80]

When we pray, God moves on our hearts to share the Gospel with people, and He touches the hearts of the listeners to receive the Gospel. Evangelism without prayer is like throwing seeds on concrete and hoping they grow into an orchard.

Talk to Jesus about your friends before you talk to your friends about Jesus. Prayer is the secret weapon of evangelism because it softens people's hearts to receive the Gospel.

And what is at the core of this Jesus movement? Jesus' heart for His family of believers could not have been any clearer: "My house shall be called a house of prayer for all nations." (Mark 11:17)

The Greek word Jesus uses in Mark 11:17 for "house" is *oikos*, which means family, house, or household. In essence, Jesus is saying, "My family shall be known as a family of prayer. People will recognize you as belonging to my family by the way you constantly pray for every ethnic group to be saved."

Prayer isn't one activity among many others believers should engage in—prayer is the distinguishing quality of God's family.

Think about that for a moment. Is prayer such an integral part of your life that it identifies you to others as a Christ-follower?

The Lord spoke to my friend Mark Anderson years ago, "My house shall be called a house of prayer for all nations or it will not be my house." In other words, God won't inhabit any house that isn't saturated with prayer.

Jesus isn't playing games when it comes to prayer. It's not an add-on or bonus option for believers—prayer is at the heart of what it means to be a child of God. And prayer is the foundation of mission.

What's the outcome of God's people becoming a house of prayer? Why is that so important to God?

Jesus declared in Mark 11:17, "My house shall be called a house of prayer *for* all nations." The Greek root word translated "nations" is *ethnos*, which means every culture, tribe, race, nation, and people group. Prayer opens the nations to the Gospel.

The Apostle James states in Acts 15:16-17, "After these things I will return, and I will rebuild the Tabernacle of David which has fallen, and I will rebuild its ruins, and I will restore it, so that the rest of mankind may seek the Lord and all the Gentiles who are called by name."

What was the Tabernacle of David? In essence, it was a house of prayer—a place devoted to 24/7 worship and prayer. The New Testament church is a spiritual restoration of David's Tabernacle. When the Lord reshapes His church into a place of unceasing prayer and worship, people will begin seeking and calling upon the Lord.

HOUSES OF PRAYER EVERYWHERE

The call to be a house of prayer is not only for churches— it's for believers in every sphere of society. Jesus didn't say, "My *church* shall be called a house of prayer." He instructed, "My *house* (family, household) shall be called a house of prayer."

Jesus is calling every believer, every family, every church, every ministry, and every Christian-owned business to become houses of prayer. The Holy Spirit is raising up houses of prayer everywhere.

Prayer is blossoming in the most unlikely places—in prisons, coffee shops, college campuses, schools, factories, office complexes, homes, and yes, even in churches.

Imagine what would happen if every believer and every family prayed consistently? Imagine the spiritual tsunami that would take place if even 10 percent of churches and Christian-owned businesses became houses of prayer.

This call to be a house of prayer is as much for businessmen and businesswomen as it is for pastors and churches. It's noteworthy that Jesus picked twelve men from the business world to be part of His inner circle—not one of them was a trained priest or pastor.

Author Os Hillman nailed it when he wrote: "Consider that in the New Testament, of Jesus' 132 public appearances, 122 were in the marketplace. Of the 52 parables Jesus told, 45 had a workplace context. Of 40 miracles recorded in the book of Acts, 39 occurred in the marketplace."[81]

There are many examples in the Bible, church history, and modern days of ordinary people who connected with God in prayer, discovered their purpose, and made the world a better place. You can be a house of prayer regardless of your profession or calling.

Doctors and nurses, engineers and architects, teachers and principals, chefs and dishwashers, CEOs and janitors, attorneys and clerks, managers and hourly workers, farmers and real estate moguls, developers and carpenters, electricians and plumbers, movie stars and stay-at-home moms, pastors and children's workers—all of us are called to be houses of prayer and bring the Kingdom of heaven to our circles of influence.

Prayer warriors come in all shapes and sizes, and they come from all spheres of society. Allow me to tell you the stories of a few ordinary people who have transformed lives and impacted culture through their faith, prayers, and obedience to God.

DAVID

David Green was born into a family of preachers. His mother, Marie, prayed every day that all six of her children would go into full-time ministry when they grew up.

After he was promoted to store manager at the age of twenty-one, he went home to share his excitement with his mother. David recounts this story in his book, *More Than a Hobby:*

> She smiled and then quietly said, "That's nice, Dave. But what are you doing for the Lord?" That was a touchy question for me, given the fact that I was the only one of six Green children not going into ordained ministry. My father was a pastor, and my two brothers were following in his footsteps. Two sisters had married pastors, and the third became an evangelist. I felt like the black sheep of the family. Nobody said anything directly to me about this, but I got the message anyway: I was chasing the almighty dollar, trying to be a capitalist, messing around without true purpose in my life.[82]
>
> While working as a store manager for TG&Y, David took out a $600 loan in 1970 to start a company in his garage. It was a simple business assembling and selling picture frames.

God blessed the business, and in 1972, David and his wife Barbara opened a 300-square-foot store in Oklahoma City called Hobby Lobby. Today, Hobby Lobby has annual revenues of more than $5 billion, over 900 stores, and more than 40,000 employees.

Even though God blessed his business and family more than ever imagined, David always wondered deep down if maybe he had missed his calling by not becoming an ordained minister like his father and siblings.

As the Lord began to move on David's heart to live a life of generosity, God revealed to him that he was indeed a full-time minister but in the marketplace. After he gave his first large gift of $30,000 to missions, David realized: "Maybe God has a purpose for a merchant after all. Maybe He has a place for me."[83]

David Green and his family have changed the world for God's glory. They built the Museum of the Bible in Washington, D.C., which boasts over 40,000 Biblical artifacts intended to engage people with the Bible.

They have funded the distribution of more than 1.4 billion copies of Gospel literature abroad and the development of the YouVersion Bible App, which has been downloaded on over 405 million unique devices across 144 countries.

In addition to all this, Hobby Lobby gives 50 percent of the company's annual income away to God-honoring causes, financing the work of the church throughout the world. *Forbes Magazine* has described David Green as "the largest individual donor to evangelical causes in America."[84]

David's mother, Marie, passed away in 1975. Today, all six of her children are full-time ministers—five in ordained ministry and one in marketplace ministry. Because in the end, ministry isn't a position you hold—it's the life you live.

When people pray, God does more than they could ask, think, or imagine.

SUZANNE

Suzanne raised ten children (nine more children died as infants), homeschooled them, taught them the Bible, and tended their farm with little help from her husband.

Financial provision was a constant struggle. Twice Suzanne lost everything when her home burned to the ground. Their flax field was burned, their dog was killed, and their cow's udders were sliced, so they didn't have milk.

As a girl, Suzanne promised God she would always make time to spend with Him, but now, amidst the chaos of life, there was seldom a time or place for it. So, rather than accept excuses, Suzanne told her children not to disturb her when they saw her face covered with her apron. Her apron created a private place for her to spend time with God.

Suzanne was a poor housewife and homeschool mom with little formal education, but through her prayers and godly influence, she raised world-changers. Her sons, John and Charles Wesley, are two of the most influential Christian leaders in history. John founded the Methodist church, and Charles wrote over 6,500 hymns. Suzanne Wesley made her home a house of prayer, and it changed the world.

When people pray, their prayers affect generations to come.

KEVIN

My friend Kevin grew up in a pastor's home in Norman, Oklahoma. After Kevin graduated from Norman High School, he attended Oklahoma State University, where he obtained a degree in accounting and, much to his surprise, a passion for sales.

Kevin started Gateway Mortgage Group in 2000 with $1,000, a computer, and a big dream. The Lord blessed his company beyond his wildest dreams, and it has grown to over 1,300 employees. To serve the spiritual needs of his employees, Kevin hired workplace chaplains. He realized God had called him to be a pastor—not the pastor of a church like his father, but a shepherd to his workers.

At the peak of his business career, Kevin finally felt like he had arrived. He led a successful business, his family was strong, and his relationship with God was growing. But just when Kevin got comfortable, the Lord called him to do something daring.

"Run for governor," God whispered.

That's crazy, Kevin thought to himself. *I've never held a publicly elected office before. How could I be governor?*

But the more he and Sarah prayed about it, the more confirmation they received from God. So, Kevin ran in obedience to God's call, and against all the odds, won the election. On January 14, 2018, Kevin became the 28th Governor of Oklahoma.

Governor Kevin Stitt has remained faithful to his Biblical values and his belief in the power of prayer. He is partnering with the faith community to tackle complex social problems together.

Kevin boldly proclaims, "Government can't solve these problems without the help of churches and nonprofits. But before we can win these battles in the natural realm, we have to win them in the spiritual realm through prayer. With God's help, we will become a Top 10 state."

When people pray, they discover their God-given purpose and acquire the faith to fulfill it.

JIMMY

In 1977, Jimmy and Bob Gregory founded Texas Disposal Systems (TDS) with one truck, one client, and $10,000.

With God's favor, hard work, excellent customer service, and environmental responsibility, they turned their business into one of the largest independently owned resource management companies in the country. With over 900 employees today, TDS provides waste collection and recycling services to over 180 cities. But life wasn't always this good.

Jimmy's daughter, Jennifer, experienced hysterical paralysis in 1991, and it left her in a wheelchair unable to move her right arm or right leg. After much prayer, the Lord guided Jimmy and Janet to take Jennifer to the Rapha Center in Deer Park, Texas.

By doctors' orders, they had to leave Jennifer in the hospital for seven days without any communication. After the first week of treatment, they were allowed to visit Jennifer, along with ten other families who were visiting their children.

One of the other fathers made an offhand remark that stopped Jimmy dead in his tracks: "There are two kinds of people in this world—people who work to live and people who live to work. You are either one or the other."

In that instant, Jimmy realized his life had been wrapped up in his work. He had put his business before God and his family. He came undone and rushed out of the visitor center to hide his tears, locked himself in a bathroom, got on his knees, and prayed.

"Lord, if you give me another chance, I'll never put my business before you or my family. From now on, I'll put you first, my family second, and my company third."

Jimmy got in his Ford pickup, drove to his office, and threw his huge ring of work keys on his brother's desk.

"Bobby, I'll never put our business before my family again. Never!" Jimmy shouted.

Jennifer made a full recovery, and TDS grew beyond Jimmy and Bob's wildest dreams. God drove Jimmy to the place of prayer, and he came out a different man. Life was never the same. Jimmy's prayer of surrender was the turning point in his life, his family, and his company.

When people pray, God sets their priorities straight, families thrive, and businesses flourish.

Vickie

After serving as missionaries in Kenya for four years in the early '80s, Kenn and Vickie Winkler finally returned to America with their daughter Shannon to lead Grace Christian Church in Auburn, California. Kenn was a full-time pastor, and Vickie worked as a public health nurse.

But even as she was halfway around the world, Vickie's heart was still heavy for Kenya and the widows, orphans, and sick affected by the HIV/AIDS pandemic.

After years of prayer and with the full support of her husband, Vickie launched HEART (Health Education for Africa Resource Team) in 2000 and began taking short-term mission trips to Kenya.

Everything changed again in the summer of 2003. Kenn was diagnosed with an aggressive form of cancer and died just six months later in January 2004. Vickie thought her life was over—all her plans included her beloved Kenn.

Kenn told Vickie before he passed away, "Go to Africa. That's where your heart is."

And with a broken heart, that's what Vickie did.

Many non-profits already provided home-based care to mothers dying of AIDS. One day as Vickie visited one of these centers, a widow grabbed her by the hand and begged her, "Mama Vickie, please take care of my children after I die." She gazed over to the corner of the room and saw four young children staring right back at her.

Vickie thought to herself, *Oh, my God, I can't take care of them! I would take in every orphan in Africa if I could, but where would I find the money?*

She left that place feeling helpless and overwhelmed. But her burden for so many hurting people was no less, and as she continued to pray, was consumed by the image of millions of women crying all across Africa.

Then, she felt God's lead: "Keep the mothers alive. If you take care of the mothers—get them medication, teach them a trade and give them a job—they will be able to take care of their own kids."

In 2005, Vickie opened her first WEEP center, which stands for Women Equality and Empowerment Project—one of the central ministries of HEART.

Today HEART has helped and empowered over 600 HIV-positive mothers to survive and thrive in spite of their AIDS diagnosis. HEART provides healthcare, food and nutrition, shelter, education, protection, job training, and employment to women so they can live and care for their children.

Without HEART, over 3,000 children would have become orphans and left to fend for themselves. Instead, they have all been cared for by their own mothers and given a better future. Many of them have grown up to become doctors, nurses, teachers, and engineers.

And through HEART, over 254,000 teenage girls have been provided with undergarments and sanitary towels, and entire villages have received health education and medical care from experienced medical teams.

All this transformation because one woman, Vickie Winkler, prayed, heard the cries of widows in Kenya, and decided to obey God. Vickie Winkler is not only an inspiring person; she's my aunt and my hero.

When people pray, God changes them and the world around them.

Prayer is the ultimate game-changer—prayer changes everything, but most of all, prayer changes you. I love the way Mark Batterson expresses it: *Never underestimate the power of a single prayer! One prayer can change anything, change everything. The ripple effect of our prayers can change nations, change generations.*[85]

What is the biggest prayer you are too afraid, hurt, or discouraged to pray? God wants you to pray big prayers, bold prayers, sun stand still prayers, dangerous prayers, impossible prayers. Pray with the confidence that Jesus will answer your prayers in His time according to His will. God wants to lavish His blessings on you.

What will happen when you pray? The world is waiting to find out!

Do not be afraid, little flock,
for your Father has been pleased to give you the kingdom.
Luke 12:32

CONCLUSION

For David Green, it was Hobby Lobby and generous giving to fund the Kingdom of God.

For Suzanne Wesley, it was to homeschool and disciple her children to become world-changers.

For Jimmy Gregory, it was to build a family and a company that stand the test of time.

For Harriet Tubman, it was to free slaves from a lifetime of misery and pain.

For Vickie Winkler, it was to turn the pain of losing her husband into purpose and care for orphans and widows in Kenya.

For Governor Kevin Stitt, it was to run for public office and show what could happen when you put God first.

For my brother John, it was to transform addicts and ex-convicts into radical disciples of Christ.

For me, it was to cover every city, state, and nation in day and night prayer until Jesus comes back.

Everyone has a movement inside them—and prayer is the spark that ignites it.

What is the movement inside you?

For you, it might be an anti-bullying movement at your high school, a discipleship movement on your college campus, or planting a new church.

For you, it might be a movement of generosity or a movement of compassion caring for single moms, foster children, at-risk youth, or the homeless in your community.

For you, it might be a creative idea, a new business, writing a book, a podcast, or a homeschool movement.

You have a movement inside you waiting to be birthed. This movement will glorify God, impact others, and fulfill you. It's bigger than you, and it's better than the life you have imagined for yourself. And it starts with prayer.

Prayer is the incubator of God's dream for your life. Get alone with Jesus, pour out your heart to Him, and allow Him to pour His heart into you. Cry with Him, laugh with Him, and dream with Him. And watch what happens.

Because when you pray, all things are possible!

With man this is impossible,
but with God all things are possible!
Matthew 19:26

JOIN THE MOVEMENT

For Individuals, Business Leaders, Ministry Leaders,
Small Group Leaders, Parents, and Students
(pastors see next page, 'Church Launch')

INDIVIDUALS:

You can join by committing to pray with us in your own time every day and adding your name to the movement at WhenPeoplePray.com, where you will also receive exclusive content and updates on local and global prayer topics!

BUSINESSES, MINISTRIES, SMALL GROUPS, FAMILIES, AND SOCIAL GROUPS:

CHOOSE A DAY.

You can launch day and night prayer in your own circle! Choose a consistent day each month to commit in prayer with your team, small group, or family. Example: The 14th of every month or every third Monday.

CHOOSE A TIME.

If not regularly throughout the whole day, then choose a time slot. Perhaps the hour before every first-of-the-month board meeting, an hour at the end of your last-of-the-month weekly small group meeting, or an hour after family dinner once a month. Example: 6 p.m. – 7 p.m.

SHARE THE VISION.

Share the vision of unceasing prayer with your team, small group members, or family. Feel free to utilize the official America Prays promotional video at AmericaPrays.org.

SIGN UP.

Visit WhenPeoplePray.com to sign up and receive additional resources and information.

PRAY.

Visit WhenPeoplePray.com for a list of current prayer points and topics we are covering together or seek the Lord on your own original prayer points. Perhaps each person in your team, small group, or family brings one point to the table.

FOLLOW ON SOCIAL MEDIA.

Follow @WhenPeoplePray on Facebook and Instagram to share your energy with other believers in this movement around the world and stay updated on special events, resources, and topics.

SHARE.

Spread the word and call others to join as well!

CHURCH LAUNCH

Simple Steps to Launch a
Day of Prayer in Your Church

ADOPT A DAY OF PRAYER:
Sign up for a monthly full day of prayer (24 hours) or half-day of prayer (12 hours) at WhenPeoplePray.com. Your church will pray the same day of the month (1st, 8th) or day of the week (Second Wednesday, Fourth Friday).

APPOINT A PRAYER COORDINATOR:
The Prayer Coordinator is a member of the church, who under the leadership of the pastor, organizes, schedules, and provides general leadership for the church's prayer activities (including the day of prayer). This person needs an active and healthy prayer life, a good reputation in and outside of the church, and the ability to lead in prayer and mobilize others to pray.

SHARE THE VISION:
The Pastor shares the vision with the church during Sunday morning services a few weeks before the first day of prayer. Points to include:
- Share the goals behind the day of prayer
- Affirm the prayer coordinator and his/her role
- Encourage people to sign up to pray for 30 or 60 minutes

RECRUIT AND FOLLOW UP:

Using prayer commitment cards or sign up sheets during or after services, have people sign up for a prayer time slot. Print and distribute simple prayer points to those who sign up (suggestions on how to pray during their committed prayer time, including specific and measurable prayer points to pray for the church, city, and state).

The Prayer Coordinator follows up with those who sign up (through text, email, or the church's preferred method of communication), with prayer points, scheduled time reminders, encouragement, etc., and works on getting all the time slots filled by prayer partners.

PRAY:

Prayer partners pray from home, school, work, church, or anywhere. This will help them make prayer a daily lifestyle.

MAIN POINTS

Prayer is powerless on its own, but it gives you access to Jesus, who is the power of God. Put your faith in Jesus, not in prayer.

Prayer is more about the object of prayer—Jesus—than it is about the outcome of prayer.

Your breakthrough is in your praise.

PRAYER IS SURRENDER.
Prayer is an act of surrendering your will to God's will.

PRAYER IS IMPARTATION.
Prayer is an impartation of God's heart to your heart. Real prayer, birthed by the Spirit, moves you to weep over the things God weeps over and love the people He loves.

Discipleship is an invitation to die to yourself and live only for Jesus.

You are the most secure when you surrender everything to Jesus and lay down your life, your dreams, and your ambitions at the foot of the cross.

When prayer accompanies the Scriptures, it is a powerful combination that can lead to personal and corporate revival, life change, and societal transformation.

Jesus' devotion to prayer was His special connection to the Father that released supernatural power on His ministry.

PRAYER IS INTIMACY.
The primary purpose of prayer is intimacy with God.

Prayer is the womb of revival. Every awakening in history was birthed in prayer.

If you seek God desperately and repent of your sins, you could be the spark of revival in your community.

You are a revival waiting for a place to happen.

When God wants to bless you, anything works. When God wants to humble you, nothing works.

Christ can solve any human crisis through a united church. And nothing has the power to unite the church like prayer.

PRAYER RELEASES JUSTICE.
Justice is heaven's response to unceasing prayer.

Prayer transcends politics, race, culture, generations, and theological differences.

Serving the poor is not an add-on to the Gospel—it's at the heart of the Gospel message.

PRAYER IS UNIFYING.
Prayer is the language that moves heaven and unites Earth.

When you pray in faith according to God's will, anything is possible.

The secret to sustaining your love for Christ for a lifetime is to pursue Him daily.

PRAYER IS WARFARE.
Prayer is a declaration of war on the enemy. It's a battle between two kingdoms.

God has given you the necessary weapons to win the spiritual battle.

The two most powerful weapons you have in your arsenal are prayer and God's Word.

Prayer is more about alignment than alleviation—more about aligning our hearts and minds with God's will than alleviating pain and suffering.

PRAYER IS TRANSFORMATION.
Prayer is less about changing people and circumstances and more about transforming you into the image of Christ.

PRAYER IS TRUST.
It's not about your ability to make it happen, but your willingness to trust God to make it happen.

PRAYER IS A CONVERSATION.
Prayer is meant to be a dialogue, not a monologue—an intimate conversation between two people.

PRAYER IS MISSION.
Prayer is not the end game—mission is.

Prayer moves us to mission—to reach the lost and the least with Christ's love. Prayer opens the nations to the Gospel.

Prayer isn't one activity among many others that believers should engage in—prayer is the distinguishing quality of God's family.

Scripture commands us to pray without ceasing because God is worthy of day and night prayer, worship, and adoration.

Prayer is the ultimate game-changer—prayer changes everything, but most of all, prayer changes you.

Everyone has a movement inside them—and prayer is the spark that ignites it.

What is the movement inside you?

DISCUSSION QUESTIONS

FORMAT:

You can use this book as a 4-week sermon series or small group Bible study. You can make it longer or shorter, depending on the needs of your church or small group. Read the book individually and then meet as a group in person or virtually to discuss the chapters. Review the main points of each chapter and ask attendees to share personal stories related to the content. Encourage people to share testimonies of answered prayer. Open and close your time together in prayer for each other and your community. You can use the intro video for each chapter on our website as a discussion starter.

OUTLINE:

Week 1 | Chapters 1-3
Week 2 | Chapters 4-6
Week 3 | Chapters 7-9
Week 4 | Chapters 10-11

MEDIA:

There are chapter intro videos, graphics, and additional resources on our website that you can download for free. Visit WhenPeoplePray.com.

GOD STORIES:

We would love to hear the praise reports of answered prayer or how God has sustained you through unanswered prayer. Please share your story on our website and your social media accounts using the hashtag #WhenPeoplePray so we can celebrate with you!

PRAYER REQUESTS:

If you need prayer, please let us know on our website. We have prayer partners who would love to pray for you.

WEEK 1 DISCUSSION QUESTIONS

CHAPTER 1:

1. The book opens with the story of Brian's daughter in the hospital. Did this story remind you of any painful or desperate situations in your life? Did you reach out to God in prayer during that difficult time? Looking back, how did God respond to your prayer, and how did He change you in the process?

2. If prayer is powerless in itself, why do we pray? When we take the focus off how long and how hard we pray, and we place it on Jesus, how does that impact our relationship with God?

3. Prayer is more about the object of prayer—Jesus—than it is about the outcome of prayer. Discuss how you have focused, at times, more on the outcomes of prayer than on the object of prayer, Jesus. Discuss how you can change that pattern and begin focusing on Jesus. Renew your commitment to put Jesus first in your prayers and your life.

CHAPTER 2:

4. Brian is transparent about his struggle with sin and temptation. Genesis 4:7 says, "Sin is crouching at your door; it desires to have you, but you must rule over it." Take some time to reflect on personal struggles with sin and temptation to disobey God's Word. Depending on the dynamics of your small group, you may even consider discussing them out loud. Take a moment to pray for God's grace to overcome every temptation you are facing right now.

5. In Chapter 2, Brian begins recounting how God met him on a Sunday morning in answer to his mom's faithful prayers. Sometimes our most significant encounters with God and breakthroughs are actually answers to someone else's prayers. Whose prayers have you benefitted from?

CHAPTER 3:

6. Prayer is an act of surrendering your will to God's will. Brian talks a lot about his struggle to trust God with his daughter and surrender to God's call for his life. Have you ever struggled to trust God or surrender to His will?

7. Prayer is warfare, but as Brian learned, your breakthrough is in your praise. Discuss any spiritual warfare you are currently

facing and take some time to praise the Lord for His faithfulness through the storms.

8. Prayer is an impartation of God's heart to your heart. Real prayer, birthed by the Spirit, moves you to weep over the things God weeps over and love the people He loves. In your prayer journey, how has God imparted His heart for people as you pray? Share stories as a group and ask God to do it again as you pray together.

WEEK 2 DISCUSSION QUESTIONS

CHAPTER 4:

1. Being a follower of Jesus isn't a label you claim; it's the person you become. Being a Christ-follower isn't about going to church, lifting your hands in worship, quoting Bible verses, or any other religious activity—it's about who you are on the inside. How are you becoming more like Jesus in the way you think, speak, act, and treat people? If you're like every other Christian in the world, there is always room for improvement. What immediate changes can you make to emulate Christ even more?

CHAPTER 5:

2. Regarding 24/7 prayer, Jason Hubbard said, "We want to create canopies of united, strategic, sustainable prayer over every city, state, and nation in the world." Unceasing prayer

helps create an awareness of God's presence in a community and increased receptivity to the Gospel. Is your city covered in 24/7 prayer yet? Would you prayerfully consider covering your city in prayer monthly and asking others to do the same? Visit WhenPeoplePray.com to find out how.

3. When Elisha received his call to serve God, he wanted to be fully committed. He didn't want to have a backup plan. So, he slaughtered his oxen and used the wood from the yokes to burn their flesh (1 Kings 19:21). When we pray, God will undoubtedly call us into service and ask us to shift our focus to His priorities. For you, it may not mean that you burn down your business, but for all of us, it always means we say yes to His plan and no to our backup plans. Prayer should always move us to be fully committed to God. What is God saying about His plan for your life and your backup plans? What is your next step to being fully committed?

CHAPTER 6:

4. The primary purpose of intimacy with God. Jesus' devotion to prayer was His special connection to the Father. It released supernatural power on everything He did. Do you have a daily committed time for prayer and Bible study? What do you need to eliminate from your life and busy schedule so you can spend quality time with God every day? What or who do you need to say no to so you can say yes to God?

5. Prayer is the womb of revival. Every awakening in history was birthed in prayer. Dr. A. T. Pierson said, "There has never been a spiritual awakening in any country or locality that

did not begin in united prayer." Take a moment to discuss what revival would look like in your city. Are you willing to pray for revival and unite with other believers even if they hold different political or theological views? If you are willing, why not start now and reach out to one or two people who can join you in prayer for revival?

6. You are a revival waiting for a place to happen. In other words, revival starts with you and God. According to Henry Blackaby's definition of revival, where are you at in the process of being revived? What steps are you willing to take to be revived and to usher revival to your circle of influence?

WEEK 3 DISCUSSION QUESTIONS

CHAPTER 7:

1. When God wants to bless you, anything works. When God wants to humble you, nothing works. If you are frustrated, is it possible you are trying to force something that is God's will but not God's time?

2. We believe a praying church is also a compassionate church that serves the poor and neglected. Serving the poor is not an add-on to the Gospel—it's at the heart of the Gospel message. As Jesus said in Luke 4:18, the Gospel has a special application for the poor. How can you, as an individual, and

secondly, as a group, serve the poor, sick, elderly, orphans, widows, and homeless in your community?

CHAPTER 8:

3. We're often afraid to pray for those we love the most because deep down, we worry we will be disappointed if God doesn't answer our prayers. But I've discovered the more intimate and vulnerable we're willing to get in prayer, the more God can do in our hearts. What are some prayers you have been afraid to pray because you didn't want to be disappointed and let down? Pray them now.

4. The secret to sustaining your love for Christ for a lifetime is to pursue Him daily. Jesus asked His disciples in Matthew 26:40: "Could you not watch and pray with me for one hour?" Are you spending quality time with God every day? Stop right now and schedule a daily recurring time with God. If you don't plan it, it won't happen.

5. Practice Mart Green's method of reading the Bible prayerfully. Choose a passage of Scripture and pray Mart's OIOI prayer as you read and apply the Word to your life: OPEN my eyes. Give me INSIGHT so I can OBEY what you tell me. Increase my INTIMACY with you.

CHAPTER 9:

6. Disappointment with God is a universal experience that no one is immune from, not even those who are closest to God. Have you ever sought God with your whole heart, for weeks, months, or even years, and dared to believe in the power of prayer, only to be disappointed? Discuss some of those

disappointments. Have you been able to express them to God openly and honestly?

7. Prayer is trust. It's not about your ability to make it happen, but your willingness to trust God to make it happen. Discuss times when, instead of dwelling on disappointment, you chose to rest and trust in God and how that changed your perspective and your situation.

WEEK 4 DISCUSSION QUESTIONS

CHAPTER 10:

1. Prayer is meant to be a dialogue—not a monologue— an intimate conversation between two people. Are you a conversation hog when you pray? Do you do all the talking or do you wait and listen for God to speak to you? What God has to say to you is more important than what you have to say to Him. Take some time now to listen to God's voice. Share it with the group if appropriate.

2. There are four keys to hearing God's voice: (1) Pray every morning. (2) Expect God to speak to you. (3) Listen to God's voice and be ready to be taught. (4) When you hear God speak, obey Him.

Take some time to discuss and evaluate how you are doing with each of these. Are you consistently praying in the mornings before you start your day? When you pray, do you expect God to speak to you? Do you listen to God's voice with the posture of a student ready to learn from his teacher? When you hear God's voice, do you obey Him?

3. If you don't obey God when He speaks to you, He will stop talking to you at some point. If you are unable to hear God's voice right now, ask yourself if you have obeyed the last word God gave you. Obey the last message God gave you, and He will start speaking to you again. Share an instance where disobedience kept you from hearing God's voice in the past.

4. Chapter 10 discusses many ways God speaks to His people. Which of these have you found the most helpful? Which have you never experienced? Are there other ways you have heard God's voice not discussed in the book?

5. Discuss a time you heard God's still small voice. What did He say to you? What was the impact on your life and on the lives of those around you of hearing God's voice? Do you quiet your spirit and actively listen to God's voice every day?

CHAPTER 11:

6. Which of the stories shared in Chapter 11 made the most impact on you? Why?

7. What is the biggest prayer you are too afraid, hurt, or discouraged to pray? Give it a voice now. God is listening.

8. The mission is sharing the love and Good News of Jesus Christ with people who are far from God. That includes evangelism, compassionate service, cross-cultural missions,

and one-on-one discipleship. Discuss the people who are in your circle of influence who need Jesus, pray for them, and write an action plan to minister to them.

9. The call to be a house of prayer is not only for churches but for believers in every sphere of society. Jesus is calling every believer, every family, every church, every ministry, and every Christian-owned business to become houses of prayer. Are you a house of prayer? Is your home a house of prayer? Is your family a house of prayer? Is your church a house of prayer? Is your business a house of prayer? Discuss what you can do to integrate prayer into everything you do.

10. Everyone has a movement inside them—and prayer is the spark that ignites it. What is the movement inside you?

ABOUT THE AUTHOR

Brian Alarid is President and Founder of America Prays and World Prays, and the Founding Pastor of Passion Church. Brian has twenty-six years of experience in pastoral ministry and executive leadership. He has equipped and inspired thousands of people in seventeen countries through conferences, television, and radio.

Brian serves as the Pastor of the New Mexico Legislative Prayer Caucus, Coordinator for National Day of Prayer Albuquerque, Co-Chairman of Convoy of Hope Albuquerque, and Ambassador for the City of Albuquerque. He serves on Mayor Keller's homelessness advisory council, chairs Mayor Hull's Rio Rancho faith advisory council, and leads a monthly leadership lunch for the Albuquerque Police Department.

Brian has a Master's degree in Organizational Leadership from Regent University, and a Bachelor's degree in Theology. Brian has been married to Mercy Alarid for twenty-three years, and they reside in Albuquerque, New Mexico with their three children.

I'd love to hear from you!

Phone:
505-395-6410

Email:
brian@brianalarid.com

Websites:
WhenPeoplePray.com
BrianAlarid.com

Twitter:
@BrianAlarid

Facebook:
Brian Alarid Ministries

Instagram:
@BrianAlarid

LinkedIn:
Linkedin.com/in/BrianAlarid

**Meet Brian, watch videos, and so much more at
CedarGatePublishing.com!**

ENDNOTES

1. Ortberg, J. (2002). The Life You've Always Wanted. Grand Rapids, MI: Zondervan.

2. Akinpelu, Y. (2020). Blow the Cap Off Your Capability. United Kingdom: Pneuma Springs Publishing.

3. Greig, P. (2019). How to Pray: A Simple Guide for Normal People. Colorado Springs, CO: NAVPRESS.

4. Bounds, E. M. (1997). E. M. Bounds on Prayer. New Kensington, PA: Whitaker House.

5. Prayer will make a man cease from sin, or sin will entice a man to cease from prayer. (n.d.). Retrieved from https://quotes.yourdictionary. com/author/quote/554853

6. Dirty Dancing. (1987, August 21). Retrieved from https://www.imdb. com/title/tt0092890/

7. Chadwick, S. (2000). The Path of Prayer. Sheffield, England: Cliff College.

8. Chand, S. (2015). Leadership Pain: The Classroom for Growth. Nashville, TN: Thomas Nelson.

9. Lewis, C. S. (1996). The Problem of Pain. New York, NY: HarperCollins Publishers.

10. Valencia, N., & Chacon, A. (2013, January 05). Juarez shedding violent image, statistics show. Retrieved from https://www.cnn.

com/2013/01/05/world/americas/mexico-juarez-killings-drop/index.
html

11. Figueroa, L. (2016, January 05). Homicides in Juárez in 2015 drop
    to '07 levels. Retrieved from https://www.elpasotimes.com/story/
    news/world/juarez/2016/01/04/homicides-jurez-2015-drop-07-lev-
    els/78280942/

12. National Prayer Accord. (2018, July 31). Retrieved from https://one-
    cry.com/uncategorized/national-prayer-accord/

13. Brown. H. J. (1990). P.S. I Love You. Nashville, TN: Rutledge Hill
    Press.

14. The Message. Matthew 16:24-26.

15. Nacho Libre. (2006, June 16). Retrieved from https://www.imdb.
    com/title/tt0457510

16. Fackler, M. (2016, March 02). The World Has Yet to See... Retrieved
    from https://www.christianitytoday.com/history/issues/issue-25/
    world-has-yet-to-see.html

17. George Müller, Did you know?: Christian History Magazine. (n.d.).
    Retrieved from https://christianhistoryinstitute.org/magazine/article/
    did-you-know-mueller

18. New Living Translation. John 12:24.

19. English Standard Version. John 3:30.

20. James W. Goll, et al. "The Role of Prayer in Spiritual Awakening."
    God Encounters Ministries, 18 Sept. 2017, godencounters.com/
    role-prayer-spiritual-awakening/

21. Ravenhill, L. (1987). Why Revival Tarries. Bloomington, MN: Beth-
    any House Publishers.

22. Greig, P. (2019). How to Pray: A Simple Guide for Normal People. Colorado Springs, CO: NAVPRESS.

23. Keller, Timothy. "The Only Person Who Dares Wake up a King at 3:00 AM for a Glass of Water Is a Child. We Have That Kind of Access." Twitter, Twitter, 23 Feb. 2015, twitter.com/timkellernyc/status/569890726349307904?lang=en

24. Person. (2016, February 19). Nikolaus von Zinzendorf. Retrieved from https://www.christianitytoday.com/history/people/denominationalfounders/nikolaus-von-zinzendorf.html

25. Henley, W. (2019). Call Down Lighting. Nashville, TN: Emanate Books.

26. C, T. (n.d.). Retrieved from http://www.welshrevival.org/histories/shaw/08.htm

27. Challenge, W. (2014, March 22). HOW REVIVAL STARTS by Jim Cymbala. Retrieved from http://davidwilkersontoday.blogspot.com/2014/03/how-revival-starts-by-jim-cymbala.html

28. Murray. A. (1982). The Ministry of Intercession. New Kensington, PA: Whitaker House.

29. Blackaby, H., and Blackaby, R. (2009). Fresh Encounter. Nashville, TN: B&H Publishing Group.

30. Cauchi, T. (n.d.). Retrieved from http://www.revival-library.org/index.php/catalogues-menu/revival-miscellanies/revival-prayer/an-humble-attempt-to-promote-prayer-for-revival

31. The Lord of the Rings: The Two Towers. (2002, December 18). Retrieved from https://www.imdb.com/title/tt0167261/

32. Kaplan, E. (n.d.). New Mexico now worst in nation for property

crime. Retrieved from https://www.abqjournal.com/1070482/fbi-data-new-mexico-ranked-no-1-in-nation-in-property-crime-rates.html

33. Oxford, A. (2018, September 24). FBI statistics: Crime rose in New Mexico during 2017. Retrieved from https://www.santafenewmexican.com/news/local_news/fbi-statistics-crime-rose-in-new-mexico-during/article_27a133ae-35c7-5bb6-9f22-69abadaaab23.html

34. Reisen, M. (n.d.). ABQ metro again ranked No. 1 in auto thefts. Retrieved from https://www.abqjournal.com/1196427/albuquerque-area-ranked-no-1-in-auto-theft-again.html

35. Table 6. (2018, September 10). Retrieved from https://ucr.fbi.gov/crime-in-the-u.s/2017/crime-in-the-u.s.-2017/tables/table-6

36. Table 6. (2019, August 29). Retrieved from https://ucr.fbi.gov/crime-in-the-u.s/2018/crime-in-the-u.s.-2018/tables/table-6

37. New Living Translation. Luke 18:1-8.

38. Report: NM's Economy One of the Worst." KOAT, KOAT, 8 Oct. 2017, www.koat.com/article/report-new-mexico-s-economy-is-one-of-the-worst-in-the-united-states/5053628#

39. Kiersz, A. (2018, March 15). Every US state economy ranked from worst to best. Retrieved from https://www.businessinsider.com/state-economy-ranking-q1-2018-2#49-new-mexico-3

40. US Census Bureau. (2019, August 27). Historical Poverty Tables: People and Families - 1959 to 2018. Retrieved from https://www.census.gov/data/tables/time-series/demo/income-poverty/historical-poverty-people.html

41. Carl, D., & Hearst Television Inc. (2017, October 07). New Mexico budget deficit could hit $250 million. Retrieved from https://www.koat.com/article/new-mexico-suffering-from-financial-crisis/8820194

42. Boyd, D., & Journal Capitol Bureau. (n.d.). Oil boom drives NM revenues to record high. Retrieved from https://www.abqjournal.com/1211821/nm-revenue-levels-soar-1-2-billion-in-new-money-projected.html

43. (n.d.). Retrieved from https://www.bloomberg.com/news/articles/2018-09-30/new-mexico-top-performing-state-economy-since-trump-took-office

44. Albuquerque, NM Late-Term Abortion Capital. (n.d.). Retrieved from http://prolifewitness.org/albuquerque-nm-late-term-abortion-capital/

45. Shepard, M. (n.d.). Planned Parenthood to close 3 clinics in northern NM. Retrieved from https://www.abqjournal.com/1005257/planned-parenthood-to-close-3-clinics-in-northern-new-mexico.html

46. Gobba/WORLD, S. (2018, August 07). University ends baby body parts program. Retrieved from http://www.bpnews.net/51387/university-ends-baby-body-parts-program

47. Oxford, A. (2019, March 15). Senate rejects repeal of unenforceable abortion law. Retrieved from https://www.santafenewmexican.com/news/legislature/senate-rejects-repeal-of-unenforceable-abortion-law/article_6e90e951-af32-533e-806e-0ad7073562bc.html

48. Hill, H. (2017). Saved to Save and Saved to Serve. Eugene, OR: Wipf and Stock Publishers.

49. New Living Translation. James 5:16-18.

50. Nouwen, H. (2012). A Spirituality of Living. Nashville, TN: Upper Room Books.

51. English Standard Version. Matthew 24:12.

52. Paraphrased. Matthew 26:40.

Endnotes

Endnotes

53. Chinard, Gilbert, ed. and trans. (1969). George Washington as the French Knew Him. Westport, CT: Greenwood Publishing Group.

54. Morris, R. (2016). Frequency. Nashville, TN: Thomas Nelson.

55. Sproul, R. C. (2009). Knowing Scripture. Downers Grove, IL: Inter-Varsity Press.

56. The Message. Psalm 119:34.

57. English Standard Version. James 4:8.

58. (n.d.). Retrieved from http://www.cambridgestudycenter.com/quotes/authors/g-k-chesterton/

59. Ingraham, C. (2018, June 29). Analysis | Leisure reading in the U.S. is at an all-time low. Retrieved from https://www.washingtonpost.com/news/wonk/wp/2018/06/29/leisure-reading-in-the-u-s-is-at-an-all-time-low/

60. Stott, J. (1995). Authentic Christianity. Downers Grove, IL: Inter-Varsity Press.

61. New International Version. Luke 11:28.

62. New Living Translation. Psalm 139:23-24.

63. New Century Version. Habakkuk 2:2.

64. English Standard Version. Proverbs 22:6.

65. The Message. Ephesians 3:20.

66. Contemporary English Version. Isaiah 43:2.

67. Blackaby, H., Blackaby, R., and King, C. (2008). Experiencing God. Nashville, TN: B&H Publishing Group.

68. Lawrence, B. (2016). The Practice of the Presence of God and the

Spiritual Maxims. Overland Park, KS: Digireads.com Publishing.

69. Humez, J. (2005). Harriet Tubman: The Life and the Life Stories. Madison, WI: University of Wisconsin Press.

70. Dunbar, E. (2019). She Came to Slay. New York, NY: Simon & Schuster.

71. Bradford, S. (1869). Scenes in the Life of Harriet Tubman. Auburn, NY: W. J. Moses Printer.

72. Ibid.

73. (n.d.). Retrieved from http://www.harriettubman.com/memoriam2. html

74. Bounds, E. M. (2008). The Complete Works of E.M. Bounds. Radford, VA: Wilder Publications.

75. Ortberg, J. (2002). The Life You've Always Wanted. Grand Rapids, MI: Zondervan.

76. Batterson, M. (2017). Whispers. New York, NY: Multnomah.

77. Blackaby, H., and Blackaby, R. (2002). Hearing God. Nashville, TN: Broadman & Holman Publishers.

78. New American Standard Bible. Proverbs 11:14.

79. Hayford, J. (2001). Living the Spirit-formed Life. Ventura, CA: Regal Books.

80. English Standard Version. Matthew 9:37-38.

81. Hillman, O. (2007). TGIF: Today God is First. Ventura, CA: Gospel Light.

82. Green, D. (2005). More Than a Hobby: How a $600 Startup Became

America's Home and Craft Superstore. Nashville, TN: Thomas Nelson.

83. Ibid.

84. Solomon, B. (2015, November 02). Meet David Green: Hobby Lobby's Biblical Billionaire. Retrieved from https://www.forbes.com/sites/briansolomon/2012/09/18/david-green-the-biblical-billionaire-backing-the-evangelical-movement/#3ac7a6865807

85. Batterson, M. (2011). The Circle Maker. Grand Rapids, MI: Zondervan